EUROPA

VOLUME ONE
NUMBER TWO/THREE

REGIONALISM IN EUROPE

edited by

Peter Wagstaff

intellect

EUROPEAN STUDIES SERIES

First Published in 1994 by
Intellect Books
Suite 2, 108/110 London Road, Oxford OX3 9AW

British Library Cataloguing in Publication Data Available

ISBN 1-871516-84-6

Printed and bound in Great Britain by Cromwell Press, Wiltshire

CONTENTS

Preface

The pace of change in Europe over recent years has been so great as to make the task of foreseeing political and institutional developments hazardous in the extreme. Events of such seismic importance for the future of Europe as the unification of Germany, for example, have left commentators trailing in their wake. The prospect of imminent institutional collapse in Italy stemming from a sort of political entropy, born of cynicism and disenchantment, is surrounded by an air of suspense, but no consensus about what might follow. The deliberations of the political class leading to the Treaty on European Union (the so-called Maastricht Treaty) have been repeatedly stymied, however confusedly, by a popular reluctance in more than one country to countenance the imposition of a European bureaucratic centralism on top of a national bureaucracy. The edifice of economic and monetary union is by no means complete, and some of its essential features, such as a single currency, show no immediate signs of being delivered. The goal of political union remains no more than a hazy outline in the distance, fast disappearing over the horizon. Further afield, but well within the bounds of what Mikhail Gorbachev called 'the common European house', the dystopian fantasies of ethnic nationalism magnify minor difference into tribal conflict: unending bloodshed and unspeakable cruelty feed on the grotesque neologism of 'ethnic cleansing'.

There is one conclusion that may be drawn with some confidence from all this. In the realm of regional, national or continental identities and allegiances there are few certainties. What seems permanent is merely a snapshot of a historical moment at which, for example, the apparently solid structure of the nation-state may be only days or weeks away from change, or collapse. If, in spite of all the uncertainties, there is a future to be foretold, it is perhaps one in which states are confronted with the need to reassess their relationships, both with their neighbours and with their citizens. One in which boundaries, both external and internal, are redrawn and decision-making is no longer the exclusive prerogative of national governments acting alone or in concert with each other. As it happens, the preamble to the Maastricht Treaty contains the declaration that the member states of the European Community are determined 'to continue the process of creating an ever-closer union among the peoples of Europe, where, in keeping with the principle of subsidiarity, decisions are taken as closely as possible to the citizens'. It is in this context that the growth in regional consciousness and the affirmation of regional identities can perhaps best be seen.

The choice of countries selected for analysis here has been determined by the desire to present a wide range of variations on, and responses to, the regional theme. They are all Western European countries within the European Union but, from that common base, experiences of regional identity, and of relationships between state and region, vary greatly.

France has a long history of centralisation rooted in the political requirements of a unitary state, but modified over the years by a pragmatic response to economic needs and to increasingly vocal demands for cultural and political recognition at the periphery. Belgium is marked by a division between French and Dutch-speaking communities which goes back to the foundation of the state. This has made the task of holding the state together increasingly problematic, as the shifts in emphasis wrought by economic development have

EUROPA 1(2/3) 1994 1-2 © Intellect Ltd 1994

made a realignment of political responsibilities inevitable. Uniquely among the countries dealt with here, Germany was obliged, in the aftermath of World War Two, to adopt a new constitutional framework which established a careful equilibrium between state and regions. To this extent, the Federal Republic, with its checks and balances, plays an exemplary role in discussion of regional and state ambitions.

In contrast, it might be argued that Italy is currently undergoing a process of realignment which may well result, in these last years of the century, in a new political settlement and a radical reassessment of state-region relations. While both Spain and Portugal underwent the transition from dictatorship to democracy in the 1970s, the question of regional assertiveness calls for a different assessment in each case. Pressure on the state by regional groups has little significance in Portugal, which seems set to retain its unquestioned unitary status. In Spain, however, the emergence of the historic regions/nations of Catalonia and the Basque Country has been a major feature of post-Franco developments, so that central government is forced, at least, to take account of these regional priorities. In almost all of the cases outlined above, change and varying degrees of realignment are very much in evidence.

The United Kingdom, however, appears unchanging. Central government reigns apparently supreme, eroding the last vestiges of local government influence, both in the English regions and beyond. Yet here, too, the regional dimension to national life remains pertinent. Indeed, given the disaffection of a large part of the population, in the UK as elsewhere, with the political process in general, it might be said of regional aspiration, that rumours of its death have been much exaggerated. The contributions which follow will explore these themes, and examine the extent to which they may be given direction and coherence by the structures and influence of the European Union.

There is plenty of evidence that, in many parts of Europe, regional diversity, rooted deeply in culture, language, shared experience and aspirations, is in the ascendant, even though it may be premature to accept unreservedly the claim that 'the ideal of cultural unity in one country - everyone studying the same history book under the portrait of the same President - belongs to the dying ideology of the modern nation-state' (Ascherson, 1988, p. 219).

I would like to thank friends and colleagues for their encouragement, advice, and helpful comments: Keith Cameron (General Editor of the Intellect European Studies series), Wendy Everett, David Head and Ian Wallace, and Hilary Strickland for the preparation of the maps.

Reference
Ascherson, N. (1988), *Games with Shadows*, London, Radius.

Introduction: Region, Nation, Identity
Peter Wagstaff

'*VIVE LA NATION!*' The headline on the front page of the French Communist Party newspaper, *L'Humanité*, a week before the Maastricht Treaty referendum held in France on 20 September 1992, speaks volumes about the cross-currents and conflicting views on national identities, which presently beset Europe as a whole. As governments of the European Community edge tentatively, and with varying degrees of enthusiasm, towards agreements on economic and monetary union and the gradual erosion of frontiers, their citizens are faced with novel and bewildering challenges to traditional allegiances. Parties and interest groups from across the political spectrum are predictably keen to exploit the uncertainty in the service of a particular cause: the promotion of a particular view. Strange bedfellows are sometimes created as a result. For example, the stout defence of *la nation* mounted by the French Communist Party in the face of what it sees as the federalist drift implicit in the Maastricht debate recalls de Gaulle's vision - if not his expression - of a *Europe des patries*, and finds an echo in the reticence with which many UK Conservatives, among others, contemplate the word 'federal'.

Elsewhere in Europe, of course, and indeed within the EC itself, federalism is an accomplished fact, and long accepted as a dominant feature in the political and institutional landscape. For Germans in a newly united Germany the federal system of the *Bundesrepublik*, a meticulously calibrated balance of power between state and region, has proved itself over forty years in the eleven western *Länder* and must now show its resilience and adaptability in confronting the pressing difficulties of the five new *Länder* in the east.

In this respect, though, Germany is the exception among those countries under consideration here. In France, Italy, Spain, Portugal and the UK, the notion of federalism has no historical place in the political lexicon. Only in Belgium, with its very specific bi-polar cleavage between two cultures and two language communities, has the concept found favour with the passage of time.

If federalism is viewed with suspicion, even distaste, in some quarters, there can however be no denying the strength with which regional identity has made itself felt at so many levels across Europe in recent years. True, the collapse of Communism and of the eastern bloc has led to the explosion of pent-up regional and ethnic antagonisms, the results of which are daily and horrifically present and visible in the media. Yet even within the relative stability of the EC, the aspirations of regional entities smaller than and contained within existing nation-states have been more and more in evidence. In the space of little more than a generation, regional assertiveness has been felt in most of the countries of the EC. Whether in Scotland or Brittany, Corsica or Catalonia, Lombardy, Flanders or the Basque Country, the seamless and integral nature of the nation-state has been called into question, as regionalist movements have sought to shake off the more or less oppressive yoke of central control and to stake their claim to varying degrees of autonomy and regional self-expression.

There is, however, a problem of vocabulary. While 'federalism' may perhaps be neatly encapsulated by the definition of 'a state that divides governmental

EUROPA 1(2/3) 1994 3-14 © Intellect Ltd 1994

activities between the centre and regional units in such a way that each has the right to make the final decision in at least some fields of activity' (Rokkan and Urwin, 1982, p. 234), when it comes to nations and nationalism, region and regionalism, the issues are much less clear cut.

The concept of the nation-state is so engrained in the consciousness of Western Europeans in the twentieth century that it is tempting to assume that the two parts of the hyphenated word are largely synonymous. As the contributions which follow indicate, however, it can be argued that, to a great extent, state formation has tended to precede nationhood which therefore becomes the result of a creative act, the fostering - if necessary the invention - of collective values and myths, the building of social cohesiveness (see Kedourie, 1960, Le Bras and Todd, 1981; Todd, 1990).

To complicate matters further, interpretations of 'nationalism' vary according to country, culture and language. In the Italian context, for example, 'nationalism' tends to mean the nationalism of the Italian state, while in Spain its use is much more flexible, so that no hackles are raised by references to the historic nations of Catalonia or the Basque Country, with their own collective values, their own cohesiveness. In the UK, the word 'nationalism' is just as likely to be applied to peripheral separatisms as to the state as a whole (Keating, 1988, p. 10).

Finally, 'region' and 'regionalism' pose their own problems as defining terms. The use of 'region' or 'regional' in a trans-national context, in the form of state-to-state relationships (e.g. Poland-Hungary-Czechoslovakia) is beyond the scope of this study, which will focus instead primarily on the 'region' as a unit smaller than the state which contains it (Waever, 1993). This may mean a territory given the status of a region for administrative purposes, a unit occupying an intermediate position between central and local government. It may also mean a territory having a claim to a cultural and political individuality of its own, marked out by ethnic, historical, linguistic features, moulded by shared myths and traditions. A region may, of course, display both characteristics.

The word 'regionalism' can denote the aspirations and activism of the concerned inhabitants of a region, and can usefully be applied to the pursuit of the specific interests of such a unit. Yet a note of caution is in order here too, since 'regionalism' can often be confused with regionalisation, which is perhaps better thought of as the pursuit of state-centred policies designed to impose remedies (especially economic ones) to regional problems and imbalances. To this extent, it may be argued that regionalism and regionalisation are mutually contradictory.

For our purposes, then, 'nation' and 'region' are to be seen as key elements in the centre-periphery model most frequently adopted to describe the evolution of countries and the formation of states. This centre-periphery model of state formation is generally used to explain the process by which influence is exerted by a central point on the surrounding periphery to create a reasonably cohesive state and society. The application of the model to the countries of Western Europe is persuasive, to the extent that cities such as London, Paris, Madrid, Lisbon and Rome, have clearly performed that function of central point in their respective territories in political, in economic, and sometimes in cultural terms, assimilating their peripheral regions. It is problematical in the case of Brussels, a capital sitting uneasily at the heart of a country which is riven by the stark distinction between two cultures and communities, Dutch and French. And for very different reasons, the model is quite inappropriate in the case of Germany, a polycentric, or polycephalic, state with no central point to act as a magnet or as a force for the diffusion of a dominant political or cultural message.

And if, in any case, the centre-periphery concept is taken less literally, and seen less in terms of spatial than of cultural relationships, then the process of diffusion by which the centre permeates throughout its extended territory becomes less convincing. Or at least peripheries may start to discover that diverse cultural, social and linguistic values are irreducible to a central uniformity, and that shared values and myths produce regional cohesiveness in its own right. The revival and rehabilitation of suppressed languages such as Breton, Basque, Catalan, restores a sense of identity to regions (nations?) long deprived of their very means of expression. The Gaudi-designed apartment blocks on Las Ramblas in Barcelona stand as a statement of regionalist faith. The entire question of relationships between nation and region, centre and periphery then becomes fluid and liable to redefinition according to place and circumstance, creating a dynamic challenge to the national status quo.

In France, the regional question is thrown into stark relief by the Napoleonic centralisation which has characterised the administrative, economic, and social structure of the country for the best part of two centuries. The argument that the French nation is a creation of the French state, or of a succession of regimes constituting the power of the state and extending back into the Ancien Régime, is a persuasive one. It is hard to escape the conclusion that the multiple divisions of life in the *Hexagone* - political, social, cultural, linguistic - were systematically suppressed by the mould of Republican uniformity. The concentration of political and economic power in Paris, and the consequent centralisation of decision-making, expressed through the prefectorial system of administration, held sway throughout the nineteenth and for much of the twentieth centuries. Only gradually, with the growth of industrialisation and the consequent unevenness of development, did the disadvantages of a rigidly hierarchical system of administration and centralised planning make themselves felt. The dearth of reliable information about economic progress in a vast, varied and relatively underpopulated country led also to an element of inertia, even complacency, which was not shaken until the years after the Second World War. This was the period of a growing realisation that the growth and prosperity of Paris had drained the French provinces of resources and manpower, leaving an enfeebled network of provincial towns and an impoverished agriculture. Policy thereafter was directed at a realignment of economic activity, so that the traditional, if oversimplified, demarcation line between a relatively prosperous and dynamic North, East and South-East, and an underdeveloped and stagnant West and South-West became less clearly defined. During the 50s and 60s too, the reassertion of regional identities began to be felt, predominantly in the more excentric provinces: regionalist movements in Brittany, Corsica, Occitania and, to a lesser extent, the Basque Country and Alsace, claimed attention with demands for varying degrees of cultural, political, and economic autonomy. The twin pressures of political and economic demands led to a gradual process of regional reform emanating from the centre, highlighting the paradox inherent in a siuation where central government takes decisions relating to matters of regional autonomy. Arguably the most significant reforms were set in train in the early 1980s when, for the first time, the principle of direct election to regional assemblies was conceded. Conclusive evidence of the effectiveness of these assemblies in improving the lot of their populations and in fostering the development of regional identity and allegiance has yet to be provided. Equally elusive is the sense that the strengthening of this intermediate tier of government has reinvigorated a political process increasingly seen as stale and unimaginative. There are nevertheless indications that, at the very least, local and regional élites are intent upon redefining their relationships with their traditional legislators and paymasters in Paris. New networks of contacts between regions sharing similar preoccupations and interests, both within and beyond the national boundaries, have opened up the prospect of shaking off, albeit gradually, centuries of Parisian centralisation in favour of wider transnational allegiances.

The process of state formation in Belgium, and the forging of national identity, has been problematical in the extreme. Indeed, the attempt, begun in 1830, to create a Belgian nation out of two culturally and linguistically distinct populations cannot be said to have met with unqualified success. Here, more than in any other of the countries presently under discussion, national unity is most fragile and most frequently under threat. Here, too, the language divide is most sharply focused. The frontier between Dutch-speaking and French-speaking communities, crossing Belgium like a geological faultline but acknowledged as a political reality only in the 1960s, has perpetually bedevilled attempts to bring into being a cohesive national identity. The role of the constitutional monarchy as a symbol of unity and amicable coexistence has the appearance of a veneer, always fragile, particularly at times of dynastic succession, despite the upsurge of popular and largely unexpected feeling generated by the death of Baudouin in 1993 which brought to an end the forty-year reign of 'the King of the Belgians'.

The uneasy relationship between the two communities was further highlighted by a reversal of economic fortunes which undermined the power of the minority francophone ruling élite and gave the Flemish community the economic weight to match its numerical ascendancy. With the old industries of the Walloon territory, coal, iron and steel, in decline, Brussels, Antwerp and the Flanders coastline thrived and grew. This shift in economic prosperity stimulated the demand, on the Flemish side, for an institutional recognition of their cultural identity and, on the part of the Walloons, the determination to defend an increasingly precarious status by setting in place the territorial limits of a francophone region. A complex series of constitutional revisions undertaken with increasing urgency from 1970 onwards has addressed these issues, culminating in the adoption in 1993 of legislation which, in its broad sweep if not in every detail, sets Belgium firmly on the road towards federalism. In all this, the issue which has proved most intractable over many years is that raised by the ambivalent position of Brussels. A capital city located in Flanders, having authority over the entire country and governed by a francophone élite of long standing, Brussels is overlaid with patterns of allegiance, responsibility and identity of the utmost complexity. Little wonder then that successive Prime Ministers since the 1980s at least, have sought for Brussels the role of capital of a putative federalised Europe in order, as it were, to superimpose one pattern on another, lending legitimacy and conviction to a Belgium moving towards federalism.

The German perspective on federalism is very different. Theo Stammen explains how the modern German state was formed in the ruins of the Third Reich and under the tutelage of the Allied Occupying Powers. The constitution of the *Bundesrepublik*, or Federal Republic, reflected both an awareness of earlier broadly federal traditions under first Bismarck and then the Weimar Republic, and also a determination to avoid the pitfalls of those early examples. In particular, the relative impotence of the regions under the Weimar Republic explained the weakness of resistance to Hitler's rise and permitted the all-too-easy dismantling of federal influence following his seizure of power. The federal tradition extended also to the 'other' German state, the fledgling German Democratic Republic which, at least in its early years, adopted the Weimar pattern, only to abandon it once the goal of a monolithic socialist state was established. The fundamental importance of the *Bundesrepublik's* carefully balanced federal system as a defence against the repetition of past mistakes, against the concentration of too much power in one place, is underlined by the fact that the federal principle is unalterably enshrined in the constitution or Basic Law (*Grundgesetz*). Not even a 100% majority of both parliamentary chambers (the national parliament, or *Bundestag*, and the representative chamber for the *Länder*, the *Bundesrat*) is sufficient to remove the guarantee of permanent federalism. The federal state system in Germany, then, offers a settled pattern of vertical power distribution through localities, *Länder* and the state, plus horizontal attributes of self-government at each level as appropriate. The allocation of responsibilities within this system is complex and carefully regulated, with clearly delineated powers for each level, as well as an element of concurrent legislation which permits shared decision-making in some areas. In addition, the redistributive nature of the tax regime ensures that those *Länder* which are least well developed economically are effectively subsidised by the more prosperous. This measure of 'equalisation' of tax revenues is particularly significant at a time when the old north-south economic divide has been altered by the decline of traditional industries, and when the severely under-developed *Länder* of the former East Germany have been newly absorbed into the *Bundesrepublik*.

In political terms, too, federalism is seen as a crucial element in the building and reinforcement of the democratic process. From the origins of the *Bundesrepublik* a deliberate policy of education through democratisation was adopted, with citizens made familiar with the electoral process first at local level, then in the *Länder* and finally nationally, at the level of the *Bund*. In addition, with the allocation of responsibility for, in particular, education policy to the intermediate level of the *Länder*, a plurality of systems and programmes was encouraged. This plurality is in itself viewed as a positive value, working against any tendency to the despotic and the authoritarian.

There are perhaps two observations to be made about the German experience of federalism. The first relates to the current situation inside Germany itself and to the problems posed by the process of German unification. The euphoria which surrounded the initial stages of unification has evaporated, to be replaced by a disillusion rooted in an awareness of the costs - only now becoming apparent - of reintegrating the former East German *Länder* into the economy and society of the *Bundesrepublik*. While the difficulties are in no way attributable to federalism, it is nonetheless true that the size of the task imposes enormous strain on a federal structure which for most of its forty-year history was able to evolve in an atmosphere of economic growth and optimism. The second observation is more positive and outward looking. For the process of European integration, promoted in the so-called Maastricht Treaty and currently meeting a somewhat equivocal response in many parts of Western Europe, there is clearly a need for new models of political and institutional structures and organisation. Germany is the only country in the EC with a developed and tested federal structure which, to an extent at least, subordinates the power of the state to that of its constituent parts. It can thus be seen as a pertinent example of possible future patterns of development for the EC as a whole which, if it is to make further progress towards integration, may well have to consider ways of strengthening the diversity of regional identities within a wider institutional framework. Indeed, it is perhaps the German model which approximates best to the concept of 'subsidiarity' enshrined in the Maastricht Treaty.

Italian regionalism is analysed by Anna Bull in terms of its administrative, political, and economic impact at different stages since Unification. Early debate about the merits of regional devolution revolved around the agreed need to harmonise regional differences and a wide range of cultures: the method finally adopted, in 1865, saw the introduction of a rigid prefectorial system which established representatives of national executive power at local level. The perception, in the aftermath of the Second World War, that the rise of fascism in Italy had been aided by the centralised nature of the state, led to a new involvement with the idea of decentralisation. Paradoxically, the re-emergence of federalism as a strand of political thought coincides with the attainment by Italy of a greater sense of cultural and linguistic homogeneity than at any previous period. Other factors, therefore, create a specifically Italian environment in which federalism and regional preoccupations can flourish. These include, above all, the corrupt nature of the relationship between the political and business worlds, organised crime, and the general deterioration of political institutions, all serving to induce cynicism on the part of the electorate and a desire for systematic institutional change. The Northern League's proposal for a federal state made up of three macro-regions (North, Centre, South) won an unexpected level of electoral support at the beginning of the 1990s and, with the disarray to which the Socialist and Christian Democratic parties have been condemned by the recent corruption scandals, appears to have set part at least of the political agenda for the immediate future.

Throughout much of the twentieth century, attempts have been made to address the problem of the under-development of southern Italy. The two-way process of state subsidies in return for electoral support was a constant feature of the political scene. Attempts to help first agriculture and then industry, through the centralised agency of the *Cassa per il Mezzogiorno* had limited success, with problems blamed on excessive centralisation, yet subsequent attempts to devolve responsibility became mired in the ever-present corruption and clientelism. Accordingly, the concept of regional development in itself has been called into question by Northerners resentful of the need to subsidise the South, and this resentment can be seen as responsible in part for the federalist proposals of the Northern League. Legislation enacted in 1990 to regulate relations between central, regional, and local government appears to assign superior powers to the regions in planning terms, and yet federalist demands persist. The Northern League's macro-region proposals have no support from the Northern regions themselves, which base their own ideas on the model of the German *Länder*. It is clear, however, that, should the views of the League and the regions converge, a major and perhaps irresistible force for change would be created. Popular support for institutional change, embracing regional reform, was indicated by the results of a number of referenda held in 1993, although the speed at which political developments have occurred during this period make the future highly unpredictable. It seems clear, however, that the regional divide is a permanent feature of the Italian political landscape. It is less clear whether this lanmdscape will eventually contain the elements of a federal state or even a more radical regionalist system.

European integration receives broad support from the Italian population as a whole: indeed, innovative political groupings such as the Northern League see the European dimension as an ideal context for the renewal of contact between Northern Italy and its trans-alpine neighbours. At an economic level, trans-national and interregional collaborative agreements have met with wide support. The conclusion is, however, unavoidable, that Italian enthusiasm for many or all aspects of European integration may have less to do with trans-national solidarity and idealism than with a widespread distrust of and frustration with central government. It is the perceived inadequacies of a particular - Italian - form of the nation-state that explain the appeal of an as yet ill-defined federal Europe.

Allan Williams offers two sharply contrasting images of the regional question in the Iberian peninsular. He traces the origins of the contrast to the difference in the process of state formation in Spain and Portugal respectively. In more than five hundred years, the supremacy of the Portuguese state has remained virtually unchallenged by any of its regions. This is attributable to the fact that the state, formed by military conquest over the Moors from the fourteenth century, preceded the nation, which duly found its identity, and created its myths, in the challenge and opportunities of its Atlantic seaboard. Discovery, conquest and the founding of colonies brought unity and a sense of shared purpose. Furthermore, the ubiquity of the Portuguese language throughout the territory has cemented that unity, underlining once more the central importance of a distinctive language as an indicator of cultural limits and thus of national identity. Other factors also impinge on Portuguese nationhood to various degrees: an urban network in which the influence of Lisbon is preponderant; the pervasive influence of political and economic élites from the urban bourgeoisie and their gravitation towards the capital: these are all factors which go some way to explaining the homogeneity of the Portuguese state. Clearly, the half century of dictatorship under Salazar confirmed and reinforced this seamless national identity, with its high degree of centralised, corporatist control and minimal financial power at local government level. Even after the transition to democracy in the mid-1970s, however, tentative plans for a regional administration stayed very much in the shadow of a reinvigorated local, municipal, government, fostering the view that the size and uniformity of the country as a whole does not justify an additional, intermediate, tier. The sole exception to the state's unquestioned supremacy has been evident periodically in the Atlantic islands, but the granting of directly-elected assemblies to the Azores and Madeira, with the power to raise local taxes, in the post-Salazar era has largely defused the impact of their regionalist movements, despite the islands' reliance on Lisbon for budgetary supplementation.

In Spain, however, the picture is very different. Successive waves of separatist activity since the early nineteenth century form a backcloth for modern regionalist aspirations. State formation in Spain has a long history, and is rooted in both military conquest and alliances through royal marriages. This latter feature ensured, in contrast to the situation in Portugal, the persistence of a variety of regional identities outside centralised Castille. Ancient rights, notably in the Basque country and Catalonia, coupled with uneven economic development from the very beginnings of industrialisation, led to regionalist pressures from the late nineteenth century, and to the restoration of a measure of autonomy in the three historic minority nations, Catalonia, the Basque Country and Galicia, in the early decades of the twentieth. Subsequently, the Franco regime eradicated all traces of regionalism, but failed to expunge the desire for it, so that, on Franco's death, demands for regional recognition and reform were loud and persistent. A number of factors provide an explanation for the strength of these demands. The most far-reaching and fundamental of these is cultural difference, exemplified by the language factor, which differentiates and identifies Catalans, Basques, and Galicians. Castillian Spanish is spoken by no more than three quarters of the population of Spain as a whole, with the result that the three minorities and, in particular, large cities such as Barcelona or Bilbao, exert a centrifugal force, encouraging the growth of regionalisms and thus of a society with a number of different focal points.

Cultural difference was amplified in the mid-twentieth century by starkly uneven economic development. With the country's political centre, Madrid, relatively undynamic in economic terms, two of the three industrially active regions – the Basque Country and Catalonia – had formed the powerhouse of early industrial development. Much of western, central and southern Spain remained undeveloped and poor. The negative effects of this pattern of development were multiple: imbalances were accentuated by migration from poor to prosperous regions; the poorest regions posed problems when the time came to create some form of regional equity, and the successful regions such as Catalonia objected to subsidising their less successful neighbours. Paradoxically, Franco's regime itself offered succour to the regionalist movements, to the extent that its heavy-handed suppression of regional activity encouraged a spirit of anti-government solidarity between regionalist movements. With the return to democracy in the post-Franco era, a measure of autonomy was seen as an essential element of constitutional reform, but its implementation posed a number of problems, not least in that some regions were obviously self-defining and eager to assume an autonomous role, while elsewhere it was by no means clear what, in precise territorial terms, constituted a region. The principles of state unity, regional autonomy, and interregional solidarity enshrined in the 1978 Constitution represented an attempt to deal pragmatically with widely divergent levels of concern. Subsequent legislation, and regional elections, have gone some way towards producing an equitable settlement which, despite its lacunae and drawbacks, has brought about in less than twenty years an astonishing degree of regional reform. Reservations remain about the strength of regional identity in some parts of the country, although the very process of reform has had the effect of raising regional consciousness in, for example, La Rioja and Cantabria.

Notions of allegiance and identity are difficult to define and assess, but the attachment of both the Spanish and Portuguese people to the idea of a European identity seems consistently high. However, it is clear that, while this attachment is actively encouraged by, and tends to be channelled through, existing regionalist movements in Spain, Portugal's unity as a nation-state is likely to remain unchallenged.

It is perhaps tempting to make a similar comment in relation to the United Kingdom. At first glance it may appear that, in the UK, the political climate is less favourable to the cause of regionalism than in almost any of the other countries under discussion in earlier chapters. Yet, Alan Butt Philip argues, a dismissive reaction to the issue of regionalism reveals more about the lack of regional awareness among the opinion formers of southern Britain than it does about the merits of the regionalist cause itself. The situation is further complicated by the tendency to focus on the nationalist demands of Scotland, Wales and Northern Ireland, at the expense of arguments in favour of the creation of regionalist institutions within England. This complexity in itself explains the reluctance of successive UK governments to become enmeshed in arguments about regionalism. The protracted debate on devolution during the 1970s, prompted in part by the growth of electoral support since the 1950s for 'minority' parties, all with some form of commitment to regional devolution, proved inconclusive. The failure of proposals for legislative devolution for Scotland and administrative devolution for Wales revealed the problems involved in ignoring the English dimension. The Conservative government of 1979 effectively removed the entire subject from the political agenda.

Regional policy in the United Kingdom, with its origins in the 1930s, has, in contrast to the emphasis in other European countries on land use and infrastructure development, been pursued with the primary objective of maintaining or creating employment. It is hardly surprising, then, that in the years since 1979, Conservative ideology has been opposed to such interventionist tactics, and regional policy has thus been accorded a low priority. Only in Scotland, Wales and Northern Ireland, where regional development agencies have worked in concert with the regional departments of central government, has it been possible for policy to evolve beyond the scrutiny of central government, often to the envy of the English regions.

One effect of the dismantling of a regional tier of administration in the UK since the early 1980s has been the need for local authorities to become fully aware of the opportunities offered to them by the regional policies of the European Community, providing a conduit for the submission of subsidy applications and requests for support from EC structural funds, conversion programmes and the like. Ironically, the European Commission appears from a certain perspective to understand regional needs and aspirations better than central government in Whitehall.

The apparent homogeneity of British society, underscored by nationally-organised mass media, can in fact be seen as a veneer concealing a bewildering diversity, in terms of origins, geography, language, religious observance, popular culture and the arts. In all, a multiple picture emerges of regions in the United Kingdom. There is a clear recognition of the distinctiveness of Scotland, Wales and Northern Ireland, while in England the absence of any sharply defined regional administration masks the existence of age-old local identities rooted in administrative and socio-cultural traditions which can be traced back for a thousand years.

However, a political culture founded on the belief in firm central government as a prerequisite for the survival of the state and the reinforcement of British power throughout the world has left little room for the concrete, institutional expression of diversity. This, coupled with a predictable reluctance on the part of the Westminster-based élites to put their own authority at risk, has ensured that the regionalist debate has been largely conducted at the margins of British political life. It may be argued, nonetheless, that the strains which exist within the British political system are such that the regional dimension can never be entirely ignored, and that external pressures exerted by the EC can be used to oblige national government to take account of regional needs.

Yet the categories of allegiance, the sense of communal belonging, which arouse the enthusiasm of peoples are not immutable. Nor are they susceptible to easy definition, their origins, as often as not, lost in the mists of time. A consistent theme to emerge from the various essays in this volume is that of contrast between, on the one hand, state formation, the process by which communities, provinces, regions can be fashioned into cohesive entities, able to be governed and administered and, on the other, the search for regional identity, the assertion of diversity. Military conquest, political and dynastic treaties and alliances, are the tools which permit or make necessary the process of state creation. Centralisation of power, often perceived from the margins as internal colonialism, is the factor which provokes regional dissent and the desire for a distinctive voice.

A further theme which recurs in the discussion of regional identities and regional politics is that of a movement away from standard centre-periphery relationships, with their self-perpetuating, oscillating tensions between state and region. It is a movement which can perhaps best be seen as the attempt to define a new regionalism, putting to one side the dictates of national allegiance, seeking to create new, trans-border regions, forming political, cultural, economic networks.

Such networks clearly find favour, particularly in the more obviously peripheral regions of the states under consideration here. The Mediterranean arc which links Catalonia with Piedmont and Lombardy via the southern French territory of Occitania; the Atlantic arc which brings together Wales, Brittany, Aquitaine, Galicia and establishes common cause between the maritime towns of Oporto, Bilbao, Nantes and Milford Haven; Anglo-Franco-Flemish declarations of common economic and social interest: all these ventures bear witness (for all their occasionally implausible connections) to the desire to create new ways of belonging. Unlike the nation or the region, however, these newly-conceived trans-border regional networks suffer from one serious lack: their very newness deprives them of a clear identity and makes it hard for them to arouse in their populations any sense of belonging or allegiance. Any attempt to forge new identities, new patterns of allegiance, must take these needs into account (Smith, 1992, p. 73).

What are the factors that govern the sense of belonging? How is the identity, and hence the allegiance, of an individual, or of a community, determined? There are perhaps two principle sets of criteria to be taken into account. First, identity lies in memory, the individual memory of a past life and experience, the collective memory of tradition, shared belief, myths, symbols, expressed in culture, ritual, language. The classic regions and nations which feature in this book patently conform, in varying degrees, to many if not all of these criteria. The second concerns the definition of identity by reference to an external reality: the individual, the collectivity, has an identity defined in part by its limits, by what it is not, by the Other. Here again, region and nation fit the pattern, the nation consolidating its form by contrast or conflict with its neighbour(s), the region by asserting itself in relation to its centralising state.

Both definitions call into question the identity of new formations. As they depend on the accumulation of remembered experience, they offer no obvious support for those structures which reach tentatively into new areas and attempt to create new patterns. Transborder regions have no easily reconstituted history, no common language or shared mythology. Even more amorphous is the overarching concept of a European identity, founded on a Babel-like confusion of signs and traditions. The only collective memories held in common by the nations and regions of Europe are memories of strife and bloodshed. Little wonder then that, in large measure, the people of Europe hesitate to embrace a European identity, when there is such an enormous gap between the fine, utopian ambition of supranational allegiance and the mundane hotchpotch of Regional Development Funds, European Social Funds, Orientation and Farming Support Funds, and the like.

There are dangers here. The exhortation to participate in a European future risks the creation of an identity vacuum, or at least an insecurity which, particularly in times of economic recession, reduces the sense of identity to the level of tribalism, an atavistic instinct which asserts itself against others in the crudest way. The growing support in recent years for the Extreme Right throughout Western Europe, and particularly in France, Belgium and Germany, stimulated in part, at least, by the perceived threat of mass migrations from the South and East, is evidence enough of the trend.

There is, though, a more positive aspect. The same mobility which brings about the clash of cultures and living standards also ensures that, increasingly, individuals have an interest or a stake in a variety of communities, large and small. Overlapping circles of allegiance, networks of belonging, are perhaps the most appropriate way to describe the formation of identity in late twentieth-century Europe. In true post-modern fashion, everyone can be many things simultaneously: 'baker, railway enthusiast, mother, conservative, from Hamburg' (Waever, 1993, p. 207). Of course that has, in many respects, always been the case. Throughout much of the nineteenth and twentieth centuries, however, it is the single category of nationality that has held sway, and that continues to exert both influence and appeal over the people of Europe, waxing and waning according to time, place and the vicissitudes of the economic cycle like the gravitational pull of some moon in its elliptical orbit, stronger then weaker as the seasons pass. It is tempting to conclude, nonetheless, that many smaller moons are also visible, with orbits which overlap without undue risk of collision, producing patterns and relationships which permit multiple allegiances and a form of belonging not insensitive to neighbouring influences and the existence of others.

References

Keating, M. (1988), *State and Regional Nationalism: Territorial Politics and the European State*, London, Harvester-Wheatsheaf.

Kedourie, E. (1960), *Nationalism*, London, Hutchinson.

Le Bras, H. and E. Todd (1981), *L'Invention de la France: atlas anthropologique et politique*, Paris, Librairie Générale Française.

Todd, E. (1990), *L'Invention de l'Europe*, Paris, Seuil.

Rokkan, S. and D.W. Urwin (eds.) (1982), *The Politics of Territorial Identity: Studies in European Regionalism*, London, Sage.

Smith, A. D. (1992), 'National identity and the idea of European unity', *International Affairs*, 68 (1), pp. 55-76 (p. 73).

Waever, O. (1993), 'Europe since 1945: crisis to renewal', in van der Dussen, J. and K. Wilson (eds.), *The History of the Idea of Europe*, Milton Keynes, The Open University.

Regionalism in France
Peter Wagstaff

1. Introduction

For much of the modern history of France, the relationship between regionalism and nationalism has appeared one-sided. References to the 'indivisible Republic' have been a commonplace of constitutional texts over two centuries, as successive regimes have sought to affirm and to strengthen the integral, seamless nature of the French state. This long-standing desire to achieve as close as possible an identification of state with nation has meant that regional diversity has been neglected, even forced to the margins of French political discourse. And yet this diversity, which has thus been seen as, at best, irrelevant and, at worst, inimical to the health and prosperity of the state, is obvious to even the most casual observer. Considered in terms of geography, climate, demography, culture, language, economy, France presents an image, or indeed a series of kaleidoscopic images, as varied as any country in Western Europe. Increasingly, in recent years, this evident diversity sits uneasily beside the notion of the monolithic 'République indivisible'.

However, alongside this insistent, at times repressive, assertion of national integrity, there is no shortage of evidence of thriving regional and local identities, nor of the popular tendency to feel most at ease with a local, as opposed to a national, allegiance. Attempts made during the nineteenth century to evaluate the citizen's feelings for the nation drew so little response, especially in the provinces, that the very notion of France as an entity could seem alien (Zeldin, 1977, p. 3), and more modern and better organised soundings of opinion have generally identified the local (town, *commune*), as opposed to the national, as the focus of a sense of belonging (Lanversin, 1989, p. 78).

There is, then, an underlying and persistent tension between regionalism and nationalism in France. The terms of this tension have remained largely unaltered since the Revolution of 1789, which laid bare the question of the opposition between, on the one hand, the dictates of national unity and the principle of equality and, on the other, the demands of individual, hence local, freedom (Schmidt, 1991, p. 4). Every shift between centralising nationalism and decentralising regionalism that has taken place in France in the last two hundred years has been fashioned in the context of that tension. Those shifts that have occurred during that period have been concentrated almost entirely in the last forty years, and indeed it could be argued that the only reforms to the administrative structure of France which have seemed likely seriously to threaten centralised national power have been those enacted during the first presidential mandate of François Mitterrand, and specifically in the law of July 1982. While the extent and radical nature of those reforms should not be overstated, they at first took many observers by surprise, and the slow process of consolidation and refinement in the years that followed says much about the ambivalence of attitudes among the governing élites.

The decentralising zeal of élites in possession of centralised power was already viewed with scepticism early in the nineteenth century, when Alexis de

Tocqueville declared that only the very disinterested or the very mediocre amongst those in public life wished to decentralise power, and that the former were rare, the latter powerless (Brongniart, 1971, p. 41). A much-reprinted newspaper cartoon by Plantu from the early 1980s is similarly pointed in its satire of such attitudes. The cartoon depicts a peaceable little hamlet, with its church spire and pitched roofs, nestling among gently rolling hills. On the steps of the tiny *mairie*, the mayor, with his tricolore sash, is asking his deputy '*Alors, elle vient, cette décentralisation?*' The reply is the sardonic '*On ne s'est pas encore décidé à Paris*' ('When's this decentralisation coming, then?' – 'They haven't made up their minds yet in Paris'). The paradox of decentralisation measures which lead to greater regional autonomy being dependent upon decisions taken at the centre, provides a telling commentary on the relationship of state and regions in France.

In order to explore the causes and consequences of this paradox and to situate it within the wider context of what François Mitterrand has called '*l'ouverture européenne*', I shall look in greater detail at the factors which underpin the historic opposition between nationalism and regionalism in France.

These factors fall broadly into two categories: the political and cultural on the one hand, and the economic on the other. The first is the focus for the tension between regionalism and nationalism in ideological terms, while the second encompasses the year by year requirements of regional and national economic development. The administrative structure of France has tended over the years to reflect both factors, albeit differently. More often than not, however, it has favoured the national over the regional, consolidating the political power at the centre while only slowly taking account of the need for economic development to be pursued in line with the strengths and priorities of particular parts of the country. In the historical survey which follows, I shall examine first the political factors which account for the establishment – and maintenance – of a rigid and hierarchical administrative system. I shall then discuss the economic factors which have progressively called into question the efficacy and even the *raison d'être* of that system. The convergence in recent years of both political and economic considerations, arguably brought about, in part at least, by the growing need to look beyond the borders of the *Hexagone* to a wider European continent, make it unhelpful and illogical to keep the two strands separate in a discussion of current trends in regional policy. Therefore I shall treat post-Second World War measures in the political, administrative and economic fields as interwoven threads in a single tapestry.

2. The centralised state: historical and cultural factors

It can be argued that French mainland territory has remained quite firmly established within clearly defined natural boundaries for so long that the identity and cohesiveness of the nation is not, and has not recently been, in doubt. The Atlantic, the English Channel, the Mediterranean, the Alps, the Vosges, the Pyrenees, have produced a hexagon bounded on five of its sides by either sea or mountain range, a land secure within its limits, simultaneously homogeneous and diverse in its geography. It was not, however, always so, and the historical succession of conquest, division, war, civil war, leading slowly, by a process of accretion, to the achievement of the modern, unified nation state, has left echoes of instability and insecurity which resonate across the centuries. A certain hazy outline of France can perhaps be discerned as early as the ninth century, with the dismemberment of the empire of Charlemagne and following the Treaty of

Verdun in 843, albeit a France lacking Brittany, Lorraine, Burgundy and Provence. Yet it is only with the accession of Louis XIV, eight hundred years later, that centuries of acquisition under Louis XI, François I and Henri IV appear consolidated, and, with the addition of Artois, Alsace, Roussillon, Franche-Comté, followed by Lorraine and Corsica under Louis XV, the map of France at the time of the Revolution of 1789 appears much as it is today.

Boundaries are not exclusively political ones, however. Diversity is perhaps most firmly rooted in the cultural domain, in the habits and traditions of a thousand provincial communities, large and small, but above all in the linguistic distinctiveness that marks North from South, periphery from centre. To the extent that there has been a single, hegemonic culture that is French, it is surely one that is northern, indeed Parisian, with the southern half of the country, not to mention peripheral regions such as Brittany and Alsace relegated, in cultural terms, to a marginality akin to folklore. Braudel has indicated, most emphatically, that the southern half of France, the civilisation of the *langue d'oc*, with its constituent dialects of languedocien, gascon, provençal, auvergnat, together with the enclaves of basque and catalan, has been subjected to an almost colonial inferiority by the triumphant culture of the *langue d'oïl* in the north (Braudel, 1986, p. 72). In purely administrative terms, the *Édit de Villers-Cotterêts* in 1539 marks the attempt, by François I to impose a linguistic uniformity through the use of French as the language of the courtroom and indicates an awareness of the importance of French as a unifying influence throughout the kingdom. The establishment of the Collège de France in 1530, where teaching was conducted in French – as opposed to the Latin of the Sorbonne – shows a similar tendency. By the decree of 17 October 1793 the decision was enforced to conduct all education, throughout the Republic, in French, and from 1880 onwards French children were all guaranteed a secular, public and obligatory education, in French, by uniformly state-trained teachers. Right up to 1969, virtually all diplomas and qualifications in the secondary and higher education systems were awarded nationally, on the basis of nationally planned and imposed programmes of study. The ubiquity of French as the language of officialdom in general, to the detriment of regional languages and *patois*, is the modern concomitant of these measures, and reflects a consistent determination on the part of successive regimes to forge a nation from a range of disparate identities (Battye and Hintze, 1992, p. 18). That determination is expressed in a concept of statehood built around a single, dominant, central source of power which gives form to the expression of national identity, and reaches out to the farthest corners of the territory, imposing its discipline and its authority. It is the Revolution which enshrines these ideas, and gives them concrete form through the new institutions of *départements* and *communes*.

In many ways, however, the administrative reorganisation of France that followed the Revolution merely set the seal on a process of organisational rationalisation started under the Ancien Régime. With the provincial nobility deprived of power from the mid-seventeenth century, seduced away from their regional roots by the attraction of the court at Versailles under Louis XIV, effective control of the provinces passed to the king. This control was exercised through his representatives, the *Intendants*, who were appointed to administer the police, justice and finance in each of the thirty-five geographical divisions of French territory, known as *généralités*. The *Intendant* was frequently known as '*le roi dans la province*', but, in a sense, this was misleading since in many regions, and particularly in those former provincial states such as Brittany, Languedoc, Provence, Burgundy, his role was largely that of adviser and intermediary. Similarly, in the more peripheral areas, such as Flanders, Lorraine, Alsace, Franche-Comté, Roussillon, where foreign traditions persisted and were consecrated by treaty, respect was shown for local traditions in tax-collection and so on. In the years immediately preceding the Revolution, proposals were already being made for the division of the *généralités* into smaller, more rationally determined units. Indeed, the proposal for a 'departmental' division was made and rejected some years before the division of the country into 83 *départements* became a reality on 15 January 1790. This division, and the geometrical precision with which it was approached – dimensions of eighteen leagues square for the *départements* – had its critics at the time, notably Edmund Burke, who, in 1790, castigated 'the present French power [as] the very first body of citizens, who, having obtained full authority to do with their country what they pleased, have chosen to dissever it in this barbarous manner' (Burke, 1905, p. 149). However, the logic behind the division similarly predated the legislation – that is to say the intention to provide a territorial division of such dimensions that a representative of the state could travel, on horseback, from the principal town to any point in the *département* between sunrise and sunset. This marks perhaps the first indication that spatial relationships have a significant functional role to play in the administrative process, and would seem, in theory at least, to enshrine the prospect of obsolescence in such territorial divisions, prefiguring the need for different divisions at other times. As Braudel has pointed out, '*la véritable mesure de la distance [est] la vitesse de déplacement des hommes*' ('The true measure of distance is the speed at which people can travel') (Braudel, 1986, p. 48). This simple and obvious fact will determine the rapidly evolving economic geography of France, and therefore the relationship between region and state, throughout the following two centuries.

The aim of the legislators of the Revolution, therefore, was to set in place a system of administration that would underscore the unity of the nation, the equality of each part of the territory, while retaining some sense of historic geographical and cultural realities. The establishment of the *commune* (44000 in total) as the basic unit of administration, and its definition as a 'natural community', whether town, village, or hamlet, echoed these realities in the law of 14 December 1789, while the *départements* tended to reflect 'natural regions' or old provincial areas, and their boundaries frequently matched diocesan boundaries. The notion of 'natural regions' is, of course, somewhat spurious, largely reflecting a desire to legitimise political decisions about the division of territory by reference to what are in fact nothing more than earlier political decisions on the same subject. Nevertheless, it was only with the arrival in power of Napoleon Bonaparte as First Consul, and the law of 28 Pluviôse, Year VIII (17 February 1800), that we find the appointment in each *département* of a functionary – the *Préfet* (Prefect) – as the representative of central government in whom the power of that government is vested, so that the principal of equality is subordinated to the demands of a newly created, hierarchical command structure. This is the origin of the rigid Napoleonic centralisation which characterises the structure of French government for much of the next two hundred years. In a very real sense, then, it has been difficult to speak in terms of local *government* in France during this period, to the extent that the phrase implies a measure of democratic decision-making and accountability in local affairs. It is more appropriate to refer to local *administration*, that is the means by which the decisions of central government are enforced at local level. A system in which government ministers transmit orders to their representative, the *préfet* who, in turn, transmits orders further down the chain of command, is a system well suited to the demands of a state bent on military consolidation and agrandisement. It is not, however, flexible enough to respond to rapidly changing economic circumstances nor to satisfy the aspirations of those parts of the country whose regional identity is strong and resistant to suppression. The imposition of this system, and its survival largely unchanged for generation after generation, is perhaps not sufficient to explain the emergence of regionalism as a significant factor in the political life of the nation. However, the combination of a rigid administrative hierarchy with starkly uneven economic development which itself stimulates regional particularisms, provides fertile ground for the growth of regional assertiveness and the demand for an administrative structure more responsive to the needs of the diversity of French regions.

The structure laid down in 1789-90, consolidated by Napoleon during the Empire, was subject to modification during the course of the nineteenth century, although not to fundamental change of form. The chief innovations concerned the introduction of the democratic principle: reforms which culminated in two laws. The *département* achieved formal juridical status (*collectivité territoriale*), and the election of a representative council (*conseil général*) in 1871, while a similarly representative body, the *conseil municipal*, was instituted in the *commune* in 1874. These two laws form the basis for local administration in modern France. Together with the hierarchical relationships between Ministers, Prefects and Mayors, they encapsulate the complex and sensitive balance between the authority of the state on the one hand and the individual freedoms enshrined in the principle of election on the other. For reasons which will become clear in the section which follows, the pattern of French local administration remains unchanged from this point until the third quarter of the twentieth century. Indeed, given the fact that reforms in this field, whether minor or radical in scope, have always tended to supplement rather than replace existing forms of organisation, it can be argued that even the most far-reaching measures, such as those enacted in the early 1980s, are inevitably less radical than they appear at first sight.

The gradual awareness that the intermediate link between *commune* and state, the *département*, was inadequate to meet the demands of changing economic, demographic, technological circumstances, stimulated at intervals, throughout the nineteenth century and beyond, a range of propositions for administrative reform from across the political spectrum. Nationalists, monarchists, federalists, socialists, all had a point of view on the desirability of a new, regional structure. Proudhon, critical of the centralising nature of the Republic, saw the possibility of new freedoms in a federation of states based loosely on the Provinces of the Ancien Régime. Comte, elaborating a determinist philosophy which emphasised the links between man and *milieu*, foresaw a regionalism which would serve the interests of that determinism. In its practical implications, the monarchism of Barrès was not dissimilar, with its insistence on the specific attributes of each region and an almost visceral attachment to diversity and pre-Revolutionary tradition. Less visionary, more acutely politicised, were the polemical views of Maurras, who found freedom incompatible with a democratic republicanism requiring a strong centralised bureaucracy in order to maintain its power. The piecemeal nature of such contributions to a debate on the merits of structural reform of territorial administration explains to some extent the absence of concerted pressures for reform. In the century from 1850 onwards, some thirty private initiatives for regional reform were forthcoming, with another fifteen or so emanating from individual parliamentarians (Brongniart, 1971, 46-48). And yet, even with the foundation of pressure groups such as the *Fédération régionaliste française* in 1900 by Charles-Brun, which led to the publication of a detailed manifesto stressing the need for both administrative and economic decentralisation, there is still no evidence of the impetus towards serious reform at governmental level.

The First World War provided some of that impetus; in 1917, the Minister for Commerce, Clémentel, proposed the setting up of 'economic regions' which were to consist of a simple regional grouping of local Chambers of Commerce, with an advisory and consultative function. Their influence, like their resources, was limited but represented nonetheless a quasi-official recognition of a territorial division larger than the *département* (Gravier, 1970, p. 47). The massive disruption caused by war was again the occasion for experiment following the division of France into 'Free' and 'Occupied Zones' in 1940, and the establishment of the French State centred on Vichy. In most respects, the changes made to rules governing *communes* and *départements* were retrograde: laws enacted in 1940 and 1942 meant that mayors were henceforth to be appointed, rather than elected, and that the local election of municipal councillors was abolished for *communes* with more than two thousand inhabitants. Superficially, the creation in 1941 of regions and regional prefects appeared to offer progress in the direction of larger, supradepartmental divisions, but these were intended as nothing more than an extra layer of administration to carry out the wishes of the state. In the aftermath of the Liberation, the regional prefects of the Vichy regime were replaced with regional *commissaires de la République* whose role was to supervise an orderly return to the legality of Republicanism and the subsequent preoccupation with re-establishing of order and central control meant that every trace of regionalisation was under assault. Public order requirements led to the creation in 1948 of administrative regions which coincided with the existing military regions, and the installation at their head of inspectors general of the administration in extraordinary mission (IGAMEs). While in one respect these innovations, brought into being at a time of crisis and with clearly defined and restrictive purposes, offered an obvious model for a potential rethinking of the administrative structure of France, they also reflected, very emphatically, the lack of will for debate on radical structural change. Experience of the vulnerability of the state, a vulnerability demonstrated in ample measure by the events of 1940-45, by invasion, annexation, occupation, all of which had seen a fragmentation of the *Hexagone* and a loss of national integrity, ensured the attraction of institutional conservatism. Thus it was, that at the beginning of the Fourth Republic, there were very few voices raised in favour of a major assault on the institutions of the defunct Third Republic. The fear of regional anarchy, the fear of a 'federalism that was such a threat to national unity in times of crisis' (Schmidt 1990, p. 73), easily prevailed.

Throughout the nineteenth and until the mid-point of the twentieth century, then, new approaches to the administrative structure of France, and therefore new ways of reconciling the age-old confrontation of national imperative and regional aspiration, remained stuck at the level of theory and debate. It was only in the years following the Second World War that the problems - vast both in number and scale - of modernisation, industrial and economic development, and social restructuring, provoking in their turn the resurgence of previously somnolent, or suppressed, regional identities, made themselves felt with such urgency that the prospect of regional reform rose to the top of the political agenda. Two problems in particular came to the fore - one might say two sides of the same coin - since the aggravation of one was always likely to lead to the aggravation of the other. An uneven geographical distribution of economic activity, leading to ever more strident contrasts between affluence and poverty on the map of France, led inevitably to the overburdening of Paris and its surrounding region, with all the attendant problems of overcrowding, excessive demands on housing, building land, industrial development, transport and communications, and a declining quality of life. We shall now examine in more detail the effects of this uneven economic development, of Parisian domination, and the consequences of the assertion of regional identity.

3. The impact of economic development

In one sense, the division of France into *départements* was both logical and simple: the fairly even distribution of population in an almost entirely rural country enabled the creation of homogeneous units not widely divergent in size (between 4,500 and 9,000 km^2). The combination of political centralisation and economic growth, however, soon brought about disparities, the effects of which were substantial and lasting. The long period of political isolation during the Napoleonic wars, together with a protectionist trading policy, ensured that the Industrial Revolution got under way later in France than, for example, in Britain. However, the steam engine was in use in the cotton industry by the 1830s and coal mining intensified during the same period. A concomitant of increased economic and industrial activity was the growth of the demand for transport. Hence not merely the increase and improvement in existing means of transport - consolidation of the road network and inland waterways - but also, and crucially, the design and construction of the railway network, the famous spider's web of lines radiating out from Paris to the newly flourishing large provincial towns. Outside Paris and a few large towns, and at least until the early years of the nineteenth century, France had been predominantly composed of isolated and static rural communities. From then on it became subject to a process of economic and industrial development which profoundly and permanently altered the relationships between one part of the country and another (Price, 1987, pp. 3-44). Heavy industry was concentrated at first around the major sources of raw materials - in the coalfields of the North, around Lille, in Lorraine with its rich deposits of ore - and along important traditional lines of communication such as the Rhône, around Lyons, with its early textile industry. Modern means of transport, chiefly the railways, although the main departmental road network was expanding massively in the 1830s, reinforced in economic and commercial terms the pre-existing political dominance of Paris. The result is a map of France in which the earlier picture of a stable, largely agrarian, society is replaced by one showing concentrated areas of intense activity. Paris and the large newly-urbanised industrial centres in the North, the East and, to an extent, the South East, exert a magnetic attraction, and the insatiable demand for industrial and commercial labour begins a long process of migration from the rural world to the urban, from small town to large town, from the provinces to

the capital. The social dislocation which is the human reality behind the
documentary and statistical evidence is chronicled imaginatively by writers such
as Balzac, with his *Comédie humaine* novels, laying bare ambition and desire in the
pursuit of fortune, and Zola, whose *Rougon-Macquart* cycle portrays the degraded
condition of the new urban poor with a fatalistic determinism.

The transformation of France from an overwhelmingly rural country to one
with a strong urban base is possibly the single most important factor in the
forging of a cohesive nation (Weber, 1976). Certainly, the process of urbanisation
which gathered pace in the last few decades of the nineteenth century coincided
with the political decisions on educational uniformity and the inculcation of the
republican ideal which was the hallmark of the early years of the Third Republic.
It would be wrong to assume, however, that the transformation happened
overnight, or that it can be described as a simple transfer of population from
country to city. Well into the twentieth century the image of France as a nation
of peasants remains convincing: in 1914 the ringing of church bells summoned
peasants from their fields to the village and enlistment in the army. The process
of industrial development itself did not automatically imply instant urbanisation,
since much early industrial activity was of an artisanal nature, especially in sectors
such as textile production. This meant that some industrial activity took place in
a rural environment, with work moving in the direction of the labour force,
although the countervailing trend of movement off the land towards the towns
became the dominant feature, and many migrants therefore came to the towns
with some previous experience of artisanal or light industrial work (Merriman,
1982, p. 23).

The phenomenon known as *l'exode rural* (rural exodus) goes hand in hand
with the progress of the industrial revolution. At the beginning of the eighteenth
century, France had a population of around twenty million, of whom seventeen
million could be classed as rural (i.e. living in *communes* of fewer than two
thousand inhabitants), and fifteen million agricultural (i.e. living from farming).
While this population increased numerically up to the middle of the nineteenth
century, its size as a proportion of the total population fell, given the faster rise
in the number of those living in towns. The agricultural population fell from
70% of the total in 1789 to around 55% in 1850. It was the poorest regions with
the least productive, mountainous, terrain which provided the new urban and
industrial workforce. The reduction in the numbers working in agriculture was a
constant feature from the 1850s: by 1946 the figure was little more than 10
million, and this represented just over half the still substantial rural population,
and a quarter of the total population of 40.5 million. Thirty years later this figure
had fallen much further, with 5,884,000, or 11.5% of the population, dependent
on farming, and no more than 9% actively engaged in agriculture (by 1990 that
last figure had fallen to 5.6%). By contrast, the urban population, which two
centuries ago accounted for less than 18% of the total, by the 1980s accounted
for about three quarters, an increase which, while substantial, still leaves France
less urbanised than many other European countries.

The urbanisation which is the natural corollary of industrial development in
any society, was accompanied in France by the concentration of activity in Paris
and its surrounding region, and therefore an influx of population, which
imposed enormous demands on the capital. Figures relating to the growth of
population both nationally and by *département* are instructive in this respect.
During the period from 1862 to 1982, the population of France as a whole rose

from 37.386 million to 54.338 million (56.6 million in 1990). The increase to 1982 is therefore of the order of 45%. If the growth in the population of the Paris region had reflected this overall pattern, then an increase from 2.466 million to 3.584 million could have been expected over that period. The actual figure for 1982 was 9.186 million, an increase of 272%, or more than 5.5 million more than suggested by the figures for the country as a whole. This 'excess' growth was greater than the combined notional surplus in the same period of all the other *départements* with greater than average growth (Lévy, 1982, p. 64). At the other end of the scale, the effects of the rural exodus can be seen in the decrease in the population of *départements* such as the Lot and the Dordogne, sandwiched between the Massif central and the Atlantic coast, which together suffered a 30% drop in population. An equally stark contrast emerges in a comparison between the most and the least populous *départements* outside the Paris region. Confirming the pattern of rural depopulation and migration to the industrial heartlands, the Lozère, at the southern end of the Massif central, has a mere 74,000 inhabitants, while the Nord *département* has more than 2.5 million. These two extremes exemplify an imbalance not foreseen by the architects of the departmental system two hundred years ago. Furthermore, it is the young and active who migrate from country to city, attracted by the prospect of higher living standards and a working life less restrictive than that to be found on the land. They leave behind an ageing rural population poorly equipped, in every sense, to cope with the demands of modernisation and renewal.

The difficulties created by the unbalanced industrial and economic development of France remained largely unaddressed until after the Second World War. This inactivity can perhaps be attibuted to several factors which, while discrete, contribute to the creation of a form of myth or idealisation. In the wake of the traumas of the Franco-Prussian war of 1870, and of the war of 1914–18, there was some reassurance in the image of a France basking in its geographical and climatic advantages and taking comfort in the traditions of rural life. (The substitution by the Vichy regime of *Travail, Famille, Patrie* for the republican motto *Liberté, Egalité, Fraternité* bears witness to the emotive appeal of deeply felt traditional values in times of crisis and uncertainty.) The insistence on France as the epitome of equilibrium and harmony, combined with elementary ignorance of the realities of agricultural inefficiency and low productivity, allowed a certain complacency to persist. The more or less even balance between the urban and the rural (the urban population only began to exceed the rural from the 1930s) was seen as a positive strength, while subsistence farming and erratic polyculture were confused with efficiency. Right up to the middle of the twentieth century and beyond, inadequate or non–existent economic planning merely reinforced the tendencies of the previous century: most modern industrial activity (cars, aeronautics, chemicals) was centred around Paris. The massive natural resources in the North and the North-East were exploited less effectively than they might have been, due to the strategic hesitations induced by the proximity of vulnerable borders. It has become something of a cliché to refer to the division of France into two parts, one prosperous, the other under-developed, by a diagonal line drawn roughly between Le Havre and Marseilles. During the Third Republic, however, and for much of the Fourth, there was little to counter the relentless accentuation of the contrast between an active and relatively prosperous France in the North and East (including, of course, Paris), and a virtual desert in the South and, in particular, the West where, with the exception of a few large ports, industrial activity was non-existent. In the years following the Second World War, the conservative instinct which had rejected administrative and institutional change in favour of structures copied from the Third Republic was similarly at work in the minds of those who had the responsibility for the process of economic renewal. The innovative opportunities offered by post-war reconstruction were, on the whole, not taken: the objective was simply to reconstruct on the pre-war pattern (Drevet, 1988, p. 25).

There is however one factor which, taken together with an accelerating speed of technological change - a new industrial revolution - finally forced governments of the Fourth and, ultimately, Fifth Republics to embrace concerted economic planning strategies and the need for a rational organisation of French territory. The population of France had remained static for the first half of the century (40.7 million in 1901; 40.5 million in 1945). In the thirty years that followed, the increase was dramatic (to 52.65 million in 1975) and made change inevitable, particularly since the urban population rose twice as fast as the rural. This thirty year period - *les Trente Glorieuses* - saw the transformation of French society, with dramatic increases in living standards, productivity and efficiency (Fourastié, 1979). A rural society shifted its focus to the urban world, and began the process of adaptation and modernisation which would make necessary a re-evaluation of the unequal relationship between Paris and *la province*. The publication in 1947 of *Paris et le désert français* by Jean François Gravier marks a watershed in this process, capturing the imagination of political élites and underlining not merely the uneven and inadequate development of provincial France, but, crucially, the harmful and debilitating effect of Paris on the rest of the country. A capital city - *la ville lumière* - which for generations, indeed centuries, had been seen as the glory of France, the seat of industry, dynamism and wealth, the guarantor of national security, now found itself accused of bleeding dry the provinces, of sucking in the resources and talent from all corners of the *Hexagone*. Gravier far-sightedly perceived the need to mount an assault on an ingrained provincial inferiority complex by holding Paris, as seat of government and centre of administration, responsible for the excesses of one centralising regime after another. The point is trenchantly reinforced by Edgard Pisani in his analysis of the potential for regional reform, *La Région pour quoi faire?*:

'*Loin d'être encore le facteur d'unité qu'elle a pu être naguère, la centralisation creuse, en fait, entre Paris et ce qui n'est pas Paris un fossé toujours plus large. Qui partage son temps entre la capitale et la province, fait, lors de chaque allée et venue, la démonstration de l'existence d'une dichotomie considérable entre une ville qui domine et dirige, et le reste de la France qui attend.*' ('Centralisation, far from being the unifying factor which it may once have been, is in fact digging an increasingly wide ditch between Paris and that which is not Paris. Anyone who divides his time between the capital and the provinces will discover, with every trip he makes, a significant dichotomy between a city which dominates and directs, and the rest of France which simply waits') (Pisani, 1969, p. 61).

The ditch referred to by Pisani created problems which were economic, political and administrative, and responses to the problems increasingly addressed all three factors as, in the course of the Fourth and Fifth Republics, governments sought to plan for rational economic development and to come to terms with a range of regional aspirations. An assessment of these responses forms the substance of the next section.

4. Regional reform: the early stages

Three factors in particular ensured that, during the course of the *trente glorieuses*, the problems of regional imbalances and of the dichotomy between Paris and *la province* would have to be addressed. First, the post-war surge in the birthrate - *le baby boom* - continued far beyond what might have been expected in the euphoria of the Liberation. For twenty-eight consecutive years, from 1946 to 1973, the annual number of births exceeded 800,000 (the pre-war figure was around 600,000). Increasing prosperity meant that mortality rates declined in the same period and, although the birthrate pattern was not to be repeated in the following generation, in spite of a natalist policy offering substantial financial incentives to families, other factors, such as a policy of substantial immigration from Algeria, Spain and Portugal, as well as the impact of returning French Algerians following that country's independence in 1963, led to a continuing rise in the population (Lévy, 1982, p. 13). The effects were, as always, felt disproportionately in Paris and the surrounding region: predictions of 14–16 million inhabitants by the end of the century were taken seriously. But pressure was also put on administrative structures throughout France, ensuring that the *départements*, which previously had performed the role of simple administrative relay between state and citizens, had to confront the demands for services in the broadest sense. Economic development aid, infrastructure projects, investment in housing, schools, public facilities of all kinds brought to the surface the need for concerted planning and a rational distribution of resources.

The second factor relates to the widening of horizons that comes with industrial and technological innovation; the France of the Fourth Republic was a France in which people in large numbers became mobile, travelling to work, or locally for pleasure at the weekend, travelling the length of the country on their annual holiday, embarking on the N7 (*Route nationale 7*) from Paris to the South, in their 4CV, Dauphine, Simca Aronde, or DS. The first-hand knowledge of somewhere other than the home *quartier* developed a public awareness of difference, and the realisation that the map of France had a certain elasticity: good communications shortened distances, improved efficiency. Poor communications had the opposite effect, and certain parts of the country, poorly served over the years by inadequate investment in roads, railways, and the rest, lagged disastrously behind. Large numbers of rural *communes* were ill-equipped, or simply too small, to deal with complex problems of resource management. This gave rise to the process of *fusion* of small *communes*, often in the teeth of much local rivalry, so that the total number has been gradually reduced to around 36,000. In spite of this rationalisation, only 2% of *communes* have more than 10,000 inhabitants, and 90% still have fewer than 2,000, while nearly a quarter of the total - nearly 10,000 *communes* - have fewer than 200 (Gruber, 1986, p. 180).

Thirdly, and in apparent contradistinction to the previous point, the expression of regional identity took on a vigour which had not been markedly visible during the century and a half of republican uniformity. The desire on the part of individuals and groups to proclaim and to take pride in local and regional values and traditions gained a ground-swell of support, and not only in the more peripheral and obviously excentric regions, such as Brittany, Alsace, Provence, the Basque country or Corsica, but also, paradoxically, in the capital. A capital, 60% of whose population was born in the provinces, was likely to harbour among its inhabitants a substantial nostalgia for regional variety and independence of spirit, coupled with a strong if unrealistic desire for an eventual *retour au pays*.

It is perhaps unsurprising, then, that the first initiatives for regional reform came piecemeal, in the shape of private ventures: the grouping together of chambers of commerce to coordinate, in embryonic fashion, efforts for improved regional development. Foremost among these was the *Comité d'Étude et de Liaison des Intérêts bretons* (CELIB) which, under the chairmanship of René Pleven, produced a programme for regional economic action in 1952. This preceded by two years the official recognition of *Comités d'expansion économique*, formed by a heterogeneous mixture of mayors, local councillors, industrialists and members of chambers of commerce with the aim of acting as regional pressure groups. By this time, the need for some form of economic planning was well entrenched at national level, but the first of what was to become the series of national economic development plans (the *Plan Monnet* of 1946-47) contained no element of regional discrimination. As Gravier has pointed out, the phrase 'town and country planning' was in use in Britain well before the 1939-45 war, but the notion of *aménagement du territoire*, which carries much of the same meaning, and adds the concept of economic development, only appeared in France towards the end of the war, and had very little impact then or for some time afterwards (Gravier, 1970, p. 57).

In 1955, the pressure exerted by the *comités d'expansion économique*, combined with the need for the state to find an appropriate framework for its economic management, led to the setting up of 22 *circonscriptions d'action régionale*, after much debate about the appropriate size and number of the new territorial divisions. These have remained the basis of regional organisation, despite revision and modification (the original Rhône and Alpes regions were brought together to form Rhône-Alpes in 1960, and Corsica was separated from Provence-Côte d'Azur in 1970). In 1964 a *Préfet coordonnateur* was installed in each region, fitting neatly into the hierarchical control system enshrined in the existing relationship between state, *département* and *commune*. At the same time, each region was provided with a *Commission de Développement économique régional* (CODER), made up of a mixture of elected representatives and interested parties nominated by the government. With no budgetary control, and only a consultative role, the CODERs appeared largely supererogatory and enfeebled. The contrast between these initial regional institutions and the *Délégation à l'Aménagement du Territoire et à l'Action régionale* (DATAR), set up as an adjunct to the Prime Minister's office in 1963, is instructive, and defines the contrast between two forms of potential action for regional development. The DATAR, acting through the various ministries and regional and departmental prefects, ensures that decisions taken centrally about investment priorities are transmitted directly to the relevant sector, a process of *déconcentration*. A system which permitted, or encouraged participation in that decision-making process at local level, and allowed finance to be raised and resources to be used at the discretion of directly elected local bodies, would qualify as *décentralisation*. All the early moves towards decision-making in regional development are categorised by the former rather than the latter term.

It would be an exaggeration to claim that the social and political upheaval that convulsed France in the spring of 1968 - *les événements de mai* - had its roots in the question of regional self-assertion and the frustrations brought about by economic and cultural impotence. Nevertheless, the image of a state frozen in the rigidity of its structures, with its élites unresponsive to the aspirations of many of its citizens, is very much that of France at this period. It is significant, therefore, that a speech made by President de Gaulle in March 1968, in Lyons, offers a recognition of the changes called for in terms of territorial organisation: '*L'effort multiséculaire de centralisation, qui fut longtemps nécessaire à notre pays pour réaliser et maintenir son unité malgré les divergences des provinces qui lui étaient successivement rattachées, ne s'impose plus désormais. Au contraire, ce sont les activités régionales qui apparaissent comme les ressorts de sa puissance économique de demain*' ('The centralisation which for centuries was needed for our country to achieve and to maintain its unity in spite of the diverse nature of the provinces which, one after another, had been added to it, is no longer essential. On the contrary, regional activity now appears as the springboard for its future economic success' (Brongniart, 1971, p. 3).

The following year, de Gaulle's plans for regional reform (combined with a putative reform of the *Sénat*), were put before the people in the form of a referendum. The plans contained novel features: full status for the regions as *collectivités territoriales* on a par with *départements* and *communes* but, unlike these latter and in apparent contradiction to the Constitution of 1958, with no elective element; the entitlement to receive the proceeds of one or two (unspecified) state taxes; the power to borrow money. In all, the intention seems to have been to encourage greater regional participation in decision-making. In the event, the pre-referendum debate was reduced, in part at least, to a sort of plebiscite on the future of de Gaulle himself, with the result that the rejection, by 53% of the voters, was perhaps less a comment on the merits of regional reform than a judgement on the immediate political situation. The measures initiated under de Gaulle's successor, Georges Pompidou, were in fact less far-reaching than those rejected in 1969. The Region was to be seen as 'the concerted expression of the *départements* of which it is composed' (Dayries and Dayries, 1978, p. 40), rather than an additional layer of administration with a status of its own. Nevertheless, a change of mood is evident from the early 1970s. Burgeoning enthusiasm for the expression of regional identity and culture is no longer stifled. Regional languages start to appear as options on programmes of study for schools and universities.

Throughout this entire period, however, it is difficult to discern any clearly defined statements of policy on the regions from the main political groupings. If anything, there is a collective, if unformulated, reiteration of the attitudes outlined by de Tocqueville 150 years previously: those with their hands on the levers of centralised power remain largely antipathetic to the theme of regionalism, as it represents a threat to that power. Throughout the 1970s the inheritors of the Gaullist tradition (the *Union des Démocrates pour la République* (*UDR*), which became the *Rassemblement pour la République* (*RPR*) in 1976), remained firmly in favour of centralisation, a policy which, with its roots in the re-establishment of republican unity after the war, was unsurprising. The *Parti républicain*, under the leadership of Giscard d'Estaing, was similarly unimpressed, at least while in office as part of the parliamentary majority. Among this majority, only the small centrist grouping, given voice by Servan-Schreiber and Lecanuet, was open to the discussion of regionalist themes. On the left of the political spectrum, too, regional matters gained little attention. The *Parti communiste*, centralist to the core, was in any case preoccupied with effecting a change of government at national level, and the parties of the left in general shared that preoccupation, holding at arm's length those regionalist movements with which, in many respects they might have been expected to make common cause. In addition, the structure of all the main national political parties reflected the centralised structure of the state so that they were ill-fitted for regional modes of operation. This is not to say that no thought was given to the theoretical possibilities of institutional change. For many individual political figures on the left (Defferre, Rocard *inter alia*) the need was for fundamental change to shake off the Gaullist tradition (Mény, 1974, p. 394). The publication of *Les Citoyens au Pouvoir* (Club Jean Moulin, 1968) crystallised the argument in favour of a massive reduction in the number of *communes* and the creation of a reduced number of powerful regions (the subtitle was *12 Régions, 2000 Communes*). In time, however, through the 1970s, opposition parties as a whole began to see the regionalist theme not simply as a distraction from the priorities of national politics but, given the persistence in government for two decades of a right and centre majority, as a possible weapon for an assault on this majority, a means of bringing about change at a national level. This perception, together with the growing tendency for regionalist movements to create an impact on the national stage, by spectacular protest and in some cases violent outburst, contrived to bring regional reform urgently to the fore.

5. Regionalist movements

Regional rebellion took a number of forms during the 1970s. Unsurprisingly, it was the most peripheral of the French regions which showed signs of the desire to assert their regional individuality, with the reinvigoration of, in some cases, long dormant and authentic associations for the promotion of regional interests. As with the impetus to regional economic reform (the CELIB), it was Brittany which led the way, building on a traditionally uncompromising rejection of the authority of the French state, proclaiming a Breton nationalism which, as with many other regionalist/nationalist movements, had its origins on the political Right and its modern manifestation on the Left. At municipal elections in 1977, the *Union Démocratique Bretonne* enjoyed a measure of popular success, having 33 of its candidates elected. This popular support, stimulated by the crisis in Breton agriculture in the 60s and 70s, but drawing also on an appeal to the assertion of cultural and linguistic difference, was echoed in only one other French region, Corsica, where similar agricultural problems provoked an analogous response. In Brittany as in Corsica, regional activism did not restrict itself to the legitimacy of the ballot box. The *Front de Libération de la Bretagne* made a number of small scale but noisy attacks on symbols of French centralist power from the late 60s onwards (television transmitters, tax offices and the like). The immediate cause of discontent leading to the expression of regionalist/nationalist sentiment in Corsica was not so much the familiar effects of centralisation – the *exode rural*, the ageing population, under-investment, indiscriminate application of national policies – as the specific instance of the repatriation of thousands of French from North Africa and their virtual takeover of the Corsican vineyards. The *Société pour la Mise en Valeur de la Corse* (SOMIVAC), established to provide centralised support for modernisation of the island, effectively subsidised the purchase of land by the new arrivals, and alienated the existing population. A welter of legitimate political groupings for the defence of Corsican interests, notably the *Action pour la Renaissance de la Corse* (ARC) received considerable support, but outbreaks of violence marked the division between those in favour of gradual development within the law and the outright autonomists. The result was twofold – and this is symptomatic of the situation in Brittany – although there its effect was felt to a lesser extent. On the one hand, the government clamped down hard on extremist action, while on the other it undertook a number of measures (job creation, increased equipment budgets, establishment of a university at Corte) designed to placate popular opinion and deprive the activists of support.

In addition to the Breton and Corsican regionalist movements, mention should be made of Occitan regionalism, which also displays a movement from its roots in the nationalist Right towards the socialist Left but which, to a large extent, was confined to the essentially cultural and linguistic preoccupations of an intelligentsia, and only attained a level of serious popular support with the crisis in viticulture in the late 60s and 70s. Its principal apologist was Robert Lafont, whose *La Révolution régionaliste* (1967) and *Décoloniser en France* (1971) provided the polemical base for the autonomist movement under the banner *Volem viure al païs* and for his own short-lived political ambitions at the national level.

Regionalist fervour in Alsace has been relatively muted; indeed, the history of the region, with its alternation between French and German sovereignty over the generations, has meant that regional instincts are rather favourable towards continued firm integration with the French nation. Nevertheless, linguistic and cultural distinctiveness was channelled into pragmatic concerns about employment and, more recently, ecological matters, while not hindering cross-border cooperation with neighbouring regions in Germany and Switzerland.

In Catalonia and the Basque country, the existence of regionalist sentiment was clearly less significant in the French context that it was for Spain. The Basque population of South-West France is only 170,000, compared with 2.5 million on the Spanish side of the Pyrenees. For both the Basques and Catalans in France, the question was one of identity, self-assertion and cultural survival, manifested by the existence of regionalist pressure groups and, from time to time, their translation into political movements of the Left which tended to receive only minimal electoral support.

6. Economic crisis and the pressure for reform

The increased activity of, and support for, regionalist pressure groups in various guises during the 1960s and 1970s is accompanied by and no doubt influenced by profound economic changes. France's founder membership of the then European Economic Community had already started to exert pressure for reform and modernisation on agriculture, notwithstanding the protection afforded in the early years by the Common Agricultural Policy. Projects for restructuring small and inefficient farms (*remembrement*), particularly in the south and west, were more and more numerous and were seen as a way of coping with an ageing farming population (in 1980, 40% of male farmers were in the age range 55-75). Many of the traditional bases of French industrial activity, such as coal and steel production, and textiles, were under pressure from foreign imports, and France's dependence on imported energy sources and raw materials ensured that, while industrial expansion continued into the 1970s, the years of recession which followed the oil crises of 1974 and 1979 exacted a heavy toll in terms of output. The annual percentage increase in GDP, which had averaged 4.2% during the

1950s, peaked at 5.7% in the 60s, before falling to 3% between 1973 and 1979, and to 1.5% after 1980. Throughout this period, the growth in the tertiary, or service sector tended to mitigate the effects of the traditional north-east/south-west economic divide, bringing increased economic activity to towns all over the France. Particularly well placed to benefit were those towns selected in the mid-60s as a focus for government investment in an attempt to counterbalance the overwhelming economic presence of Paris. Lille, Nancy and Metz, Strasbourg, Lyons, Marseilles, Toulouse, Bordeaux, Nantes and St Nazaire all enjoyed for a time the status of *Métropoles d'équilibre*, a policy which both asserted a latent provincial vitality and, perhaps inevitably, ensured that distinguishing features of the economic life of those towns gradually disappeared under a uniform blanket of nationally and multinationally-inspired investment.

As for Paris, its long-established role as a magnet for internal migrants appeared to be coming slowly to an end. An inexorable rise in population over a hundred and fifty years which, by the early 1980s saw 18.6% of the population (10.056 million) concentrated on a mere 2.2% of the territory, was reversed. In the seven years between 1975 and 1982, the Ile de France, as the Paris region was known from 1972 onwards, having had the highest rate of net immigration, became the region with the highest rate of net emigration, shrinking by 435,000. This represented a net loss of 4.4%, compared with, for example, a net gain over the same period of 6.35% in Languedoc-Roussillon. Over a twenty year period up to the mid 80s, Paris lost about a quarter of its industrial manpower (Gravier, in Uhrich, 1987, p. 325). The capital's dominance in the tertiary sector, however, remained massive: in banking, insurance, and the all-important head offices of major national and multinational companies, as well as in research and higher education. Clearly, the economic map of France had been undergoing major change and the distinctions previously visible were giving way to more piecemeal and complicated divisions. Stagnation in the North and East (Nord, Champagne-Ardenne, Lorraine) following the downturn in heavy industry and the tendency of the young to leave in search of work; stagnation because of an ageing population and low birthrate in much of the Massif central and parts of the South West (Auvergne, Limousin, Midi-Pyrénées); large population increase along the Mediterranean littoral (Languedoc-Roussillon, Provence-Alpes-Côte d'Azur); net migration into the regions of the Atlantic coast (Bretagne, Pays de Loire, Poitou-Charentes, Aquitaine); and continuing dynamism in the Centre and Rhône-Alpes.

It is against the background of these changes that François Mitterrand opted to make the need for thorough regional reform a major feature of his programme for the presidential campaign of 1981. '*La grande affaire du septennat*' was the phrase used to describe its centrality to his first term of office. The legislation that followed Mitterrand's victory and the subsequent victory of the left in the legislative elections was many-sided and complex. Its impact overall was to introduce a certain coherence into French local administration, putting *communes*, *départements* and *régions* on an equal footing as *collectivités territoriales* and making clear their specific attributions and functions. The *commune* assumed responsibilty for *urbanisme* (urban planning and building applications), for elementary schools, local roads, water, sanitation and drainage services, urban transport. The *département* dealt with a wide range of social services (child support, health care, homes for the old and handicapped), for 11-15 education (*collèges*), for departmental roads and non-urban transport. The *région* had responsibility for post-16 secondary education (*lycées*), training, regional economic development (*aménagement du territoire*), regional transport, and the establishment of periodic planning contracts (*contrats de plan*) between region and state. Within this framework, responsibility for the universities, the high-speed train network (*TGV*), main roads (*routes nationales*) and motorways lies with the state. Underpinning this breakdown of responsibilities were two innovations which defined the radical nature of the reforms. For the first time, power was devolved to directly elected regional assemblies, and the role of the *préfet*, at both regional and departmental level was substantially curtailed. The *préfet* was no longer to be the all-powerful representative of central government, but an adviser and observer, whose authority was limited to an a posteriori control of the legality of decisions taken by councillors or mayors. As a symbol of this reduced role, the name *préfet* was jettisoned in favour of the cumbersome *commissaire de la République*, a curious echo of post-war arrangements and one which the right-wing government of Chirac, during its period of *cohabitation* with Mitterrand from 1986 chose to reverse. It did not, however, make any attempt to reverse the nature of the reforms, which seem to have been widely accepted as a sensible modernisation of a stiff and archaic structure. Additional elements of the reforms were significant in that they created a breach, for the first time, in the monolithic and indivisible republic. Corsica received a special statute (*statut particulier*), with provision for generous *per capita* representation on its regional assembly and for elections scheduled several years earlier than those for the other regions. Similarly, a special statute for Paris, Lyons and Marseilles allowed for a mini-decentralisation within those three largest cities, with directly elected district councils (*conseils d'arrondissement*). Legislation to restrict the traditional *cumul des mandats*, by which individuals could hold elected posts at a variety of local and national levels simultaneously, was enacted with a certain lethargy. Pre-1981 hints by Mitterrand that a *département du pays basque* might be forthcoming were not developed.

A number of observations suggest themselves in the wake of these reforms. The euphoric assumption, in the early 1980s, that they would herald a liberation of previously untapped sources of dynamism and involvement has been dampened by the undeniable reality of a macro-economic climate that has relegated the entire regional question to the margins of debate. The regional elections which took place in 1986 (confusingly in the shadow of the legislative elections) and again in 1992 saw neither the emergence of a new political class, nor specifically regional voting trends: people voted, on the whole, in much the same way as they would have voted in national elections (Perrineau, 1987). On the other hand, the seismic shift in the national political mood reflected in the legislative elections of 1993 has brought to the fore no obvious desire to dismantle the reforms of the 1980s. Indeed, the new *Ministre de l'Intérieur et de l'Aménagement du territoire* in the government of Edouard Balladur, Charles Pasqua, has been at pains to reclaim the regional development standard for the right, while starting to sketch, in general terms, policies which take account of a France whose future economic strengths lie not simply in the big urban concentrations but in innumerable smaller networks of activity. The intention appears thus to be the 'reconquest' of the territory as a whole, with each part brought within reach, not of the capital or the big cities, but of provincial centres of communication and resources (*Le Figaro*, 1 July 1993, p. 6). From one perspective, this approach gives weight to the objection which has often figured in discussion of regional development, that *décentralisation* and *aménagement du territoire* are fundamentally incompatible, because the first implies autonomy of decision at the periphery, while the second requires decisions to be made at the centre. However, perhaps the most interesting implication of the continuing vitality of the topic is that, wherever the decisions are made, it would seem that there is no longer the automatic assumption in the regions that Paris is to be the functional focus of activity. This perception may, arguably, be flying in the face of economic reality since, once again, as the French economy picked up in the second half of the 1980s, it was Paris that was the first to benefit: nearly half the jobs created in the years after 1986 have been in the single *département* of Hauts de Seine (Benko and Lipietz, 1992, p. 13). And yet in all sorts of ways that transcend the immediate economic situation, the regions of France have been shifting their gaze from the capital to their neighbours and, in some cases, the neighbours are not exclusively French.

7. The interregional and cross-national dimension

For more than thirty years France has pursued, in a variety of ways and at differing tempos, policies intended to reduce economic disparities between regions. For virtually the whole of that period, the policies have been elaborated through, and monitored by, the DATAR in Paris, exercising its judgement about the relative merits of programmes of action affecting different parts of the country. For most of that period, too, France has had access to a variety of funds set up by the European Community for similar purposes. The Treaty of Rome made no mention of the regions or of regional preoccupations, and the Single European Act of 1986 was only slightly less laconic, referring to the intention to 'reduce the gap between different regions and the backwardness of the least developed regions'. The Maastricht Treaty has a little more to say on the subject, setting a high priority on economic and social cohesion in the regions of the Community, in order to lessen differences in development and to enable them to profit from the single market and, subsequently, a single currency. Since the inception of the Community, France has benefited from the *Fonds Européen d'Orientation et de Garantie Agricole* (FEOGA-O), for the modernisation of agriculture, and also from the *Fonds Européen Social* (FSE). From 1974 onwards, the creation of the *Fonds Européen de Développement Régional* (FEDER) has also provided resources for specific purposes, in particular, major infrastructure projects and industrial conversion projects (in the steel and textile industry, shipbuilding and fishing). Those funds destined for the Community's poorest regions have by and large passed France by, since none of its regions, with the exception of Corsica and its overseas *départements* (DOM) is poor enough to qualify. However, from 1984, the Community has participated in the co-financing of the State-Region planning contracts (*contrats de plan*), on the basis of priorities fixed by the regions. The amount of money available for infrastructure projects in underdeveloped regions such as the Massif central, and for industrial conversion projects amounts to a sum of around two billion francs a year, which is nearly the equivalent of the entire DATAR budget. In all, these projects affect nearly half of French territory (35.4% is classed as rural development zone, and 12.5% as industrial conversion zone). From 1986 onwards, the *Programmes Intégrés Méditerranéens* (PIM), initiated with the enlargement of the EC to include Spain and Portugal, have made funds available to the five southernmost regions of France (Aquitaine, Midi-Pyrénées, Languedoc-Roussillon, Provence-Alpes-Côte d'Azur, Corsica) as well as to the *départements* of Drôme and Ardèche. In the period 1989-93, the total sum made available by the Community to France for structural purposes was of the order of 40 billion francs, while FEOGA funds under the Common Agricultural Policy amounted to about 37 billion francs a year over the same period. It should be noted, however, that access to the various EC regional intervention funds indicated above was, from their inception, channelled through and controlled by Paris. Direct contact between individual regions and the European Commission in Brussels has long been frowned upon, indeed prohibited, by central government: ministerial pronouncements on the subject, even from the government which enacted the reforms of 1982, have been unambiguous. By 1985, however, a less rigid attitude was in evidence, and an inter-ministerial committee for *l'aménagement du territoire* declared that 'L'Etat ne s'oppose plus à des relations directes entre les régions et les institutions européennes [...] puisque nulle région française n'exprime de volonté centrifuge'. ('The State is no longer opposed to direct contacts between regions and European institutions [...] since no French region has centrifugal desires') (Uhrich, 1987, p. 310).

As part of the opening out within a European framework which is implicit in the growing relationships between Region, State, and Community, there have been numerous initiatives in France in recent years to develop the regional idea beyond the confines of single regions, and indeed beyond the frontiers of France. In most cases, these initiatives exist at the level of consultation, declarations of goodwill and intent and, significantly, as expressions of inter-regional solidarity, as the attempt is made to redefine and assert a regional identity beyond the shadow of Paris. One of the earliest of these initiatives, with very specific aims, was the creation, in 1979, of a ten-year plan for the economic development of three border regions, Aquitaine, Midi-Pyrénées and Languedoc-Roussillon, in order to prepare them for the impact of the entry of Spain and Portugal into the EC. The themes covered by the plan ranged from development of the road system to the promotion of regional wines, from job creation to the encouragement of research potential. With the change of government in 1981, the plan was suspended, but by 1986 the presidents of Aquitaine, Midi-Pyrénées, Languedoc-Roussillon, Provence-Alpes-Côtes d'Azur and Corsica had laid the foundations for *Le Grand Sud*, with its own office in Brussels. This grouping of the five southernmost regions is intended to supply a forum for the discussion of common interests such as transport infrastructure, tourism, training programmes, scientific and technical co-operation, as well as co-ordinating the approaches of individual regions to Brussels. Inter-regional co-operation was in evidence as early as 1984, when the *Association des Régions Françaises du Grand Est* brought together Alsace, Bourgogne, Champagne-Ardenne, Franche-Comté and Lorraine, a grouping based, like that of *Le Grand Sud*, on the decentralisation laws of 1982 and 1983 which provided for agreements between two or more regions for their common benefit. Research, technology transfer, higher education and training, tourism, and communications form the bulk of the priorities of *Le Grand Est*. Here too, an office has been set up in Brussels. Associations such as *Le Grand Sud* and *Le Grand Est* appear to represent, in part at least, the desire to counter the preponderance of Paris. Ironically, such concerns are to be felt not only at the extremities of France, but in the capital's own hinterland. Since 1990, the eight regions which make up the *Grand Bassin Parisien* (Ile de France, Picardie, Haute-Normandie, Centre, Basse Normandie, Pays de la Loire, Champagne-Ardenne, Bourgogne) have been in consultation to ensure that the continued growth and prosperity of the first among them (Ile de France) does not work to the detriment of the others (*Le Monde*, 11-12 July, 1993, p. 18). Concerted planning for infrastructure, communications, housing, environmental protection, higher education, research, are the familiar themes.

However, not all initiatives of this kind have confined themselves within the frontiers of France. The *Communauté de Travail des Pyrénées*, set up in 1983, aims to minimise the impact of the Pyrenees as a barrier between regions on either side (Aquitaine, Aragon, Catalonia, Euskadi, Languedoc-Roussillon, Midi-Pyrénées, Navarre, as well as the Principality of Andorra), encouraging the development of those regions, and contributing to the process of European unification. In comparable, if rather less ambitious vein, the *Communauté de Travail du Jura* has, since 1985, dealt with a range of industrial, agricultural, tourism and communications matters common to Franche-Comté and the Swiss *cantons* of Berne, Vaud, Neuchâtel and Jura. The same format has embraced adjacent regions from France, Switzerland and Italy since 1984, with Rhône-Alpes, Provence-Alpes-Côte d'Azur joining the Swiss *cantons* of Vaud, Valais, and Geneva, and the Italian regions of Piedmont, Liguria and Val d'Aoste in the *Communauté de Travail des Alpes Occidentales*. In 1991, a co-operation agreement brought together into a so-called 'Euroregion' five regions from three countries: Nord-Pas de Calais, Kent, Brussels-Capital, Wallonia and Flanders. The intention in this instance is to maximise benefit from the opportunities provided by the Single Market and to capitalise on the physical links provided by the Channel Tunnel and the North European High Speed Train projects. Perhaps the most spectacular of the inter-regional and cross-frontier groupings is that comprising the *Arc Atlantique* which, since its inauguration in 1989, has brought together the twenty-six regions of Europe's Atlantic coastline, from Scotland to the Algarve. The impetus for this initiative has its origins in the Pays de la Loire region, whose president, Olivier Guichard, is a long time proponent of regional development. The Pays de la Loire had already put in place a number of bilateral trans-national agreements, with Galicia and Andalucia in Spain, Emilia-Romagna in Italy and Schleswig-Holstein in Germany. The initial concerns of the *Arc Atlantique* were focussed on the essentially maritime nature of activities common to all the regions involved. The development of ports, the exploitation of marine resources, and environmental protection all figured highly on the agenda. Research, training, and transport infrastructure are seen as the priorities to be addressed in the immediate future.

With the exception of the *Grand Bassin Parisien*, these various schemes - national and trans-national alike - share one striking feature, which has two facets. They concern regions traditionally thought of as peripheral, excentric, obliged to wait on instructions from Paris. And they all ignore the capital, resolutely turning their backs, so as better to pursue dialogue with their equally marginal neighbours, and maintaining direct liaisons with the institutions of the EC in Brussels. In addition and without exception, they stress in their programmes the importance of communications as the key to development. The preoccupation with *désenclavement* (opening out) of previously isolated regions, whether through road, rail, air, or developments in telecommunications, is a constant feature of regional development planning at every level. In 1971 there was no motorway at all to the west of the Le Havre-Marseilles dividing line. By 1983 the DATAR and the Ministry of Transport had produced a *schéma directeur* for the construction of motorways and other high density roads serving France as a whole: by the late 1980s there were around 6,000 kilometres of motorway, with plans for a further 1,700 kilometres by the year 2000 (Uhrich, 1987, 275-76). Perhaps the most significant feature of these developments is the reduced emphasis on Paris as the hub of the transport system. Admittedly, the High Speed Train (TGV) network radiates from Paris and can be said to confer enormous advantages on the regions that it serves, at the expense of the less prestigious nationwide rail network as a whole. The prospect of through services which permit North-South transit without the need to change trains in Paris is, however, a major feature of TGV plans. More dramatic is the evolution of the road network to a stage which goes significantly beyond the 1983 *schéma directeur*. The construction of motorway links which ignore the Paris dimension entirely - Bordeaux-Lyons via the Auvergne, Mediterranean littoral connections bringing the regions of *Le Grand Sud* within easy reach of Barcelona and Milan - all serve to displace the centre of gravity of French activity and to galvanise interregional and Paris-*province* relations.

8. Conclusion

It has long been established that the geographical centre of France lies in the Cher *département*, forty or so kilometres south of Bourges on the RN144. In recent years, a number of *communes* located a little further south and east, in the Puy de Dôme below Vichy, have indulged in friendly rivalry for the trivial distinction of being the geographical centre of the European Community. Even with the opening up of former East Germany, the central point has apparently moved only a short distance further east. More generally, the number of towns making the somewhat vacuous claim to be the *carrefour de l'Europe* grows constantly. The significant fact to emerge from this welter of enthusiasms is that the centre of gravity of French life, for so long the unchallenged prerogative of Paris, is now less easily determined. The need for a strong, central, unifying national focus seems less urgent. Peripheral regions are less isolated than they were, and more ready to turn and look beyond their national borders. There is no indication of a desire to embrace supranational, quasi-federalist structures (the finely-balanced Maastricht referendum result in September 1992 is evidence enough of that), but it seems as if many in the French regions find the freedom to set their own development priorities, in concert with their neighbours and in direct communication with the institutions of the EC, highly congenial.

That, of course, is the view from the regions. As we have seen, however, there is not much evidence that the decentralisation reforms of the 1980s have brought about fundamental change in the nature of political representation. Neither is it clear that post-Maastricht moves on the part of the EC/EU to give a certain prominence to the regional dimension in its decision-making processes are met with great enthusiasm in Paris. Indeed, some evidence of the French government's reaction to the newly-constituted but purely consultative Committee of the Regions can be gleaned from the decision to apportion France's entitlement of twenty-four seats equally between *régions*, *départements* and *communes*. The satisfaction thus afforded to the representatives of the smaller units is matched only by the disgruntlement of the *présidents de région*. Nonetheless France, with its existing forms of regional administration, remains well-placed, in marked contrast to, for example, the United Kingdom, to take advantage of the various European structural funds, the importance of which to the economies of member states has increased substantially in recent years. It can be reasonably surmised, then, that by a process of accretion and consolidation, French interests are likely to be more and more served by regional involvement on the European stage.

However, it would be somewhat utopian, and not a little misleading, to suggest that in 1994 the goal of wider European integration is a high priority for the average French citizen at a regional or any other level. To the extent that it is possible to discern an evolution in the sense of European commitment in France, probably the best that can be said is that in the political sphere traditional party allegiances have come under severe strain. Further, the opportunity to influence the course of European affairs through the ballot box has generally been neglected in favour of the chance to pass interim and scathing judgement on the party in power nationally. Thus it is that the results of the European elections of June 1994 indicate fragmentation on the left and right of the political spectrum with support for the government list in particular leaching away to the advantage of a right-wing, anti-Maastricht grouping. A further indication of tepid support for the achievements and ambitions of the European Union can be gauged by the fact that although voter turnout in France was slightly higher than at the previous European election in 1989, it was lower than at local elections held earlier in 1994. In the short term it seems likely that the mood of the French, as reflected in their electoral choices, will remain predominantly nationalist, even parochial. In this, of course, France is by no means alone.

References:

Battye, A. and M.-A. Hintze (1992), *The French Language Today*, London, Routledge.

Benko, G. and A. Lipietz (eds.) (1992), *Les Régions qui gagnent: districts et réseaux: les nouveaux paradigmes de la géographie économique*, Paris, PUF.

Braudel, F. (1986), *L'Identité de la France: espace et histoire*, Paris, Arthaud-Flammarion.

Brongniart, P. (1971), *La Région en France*, Paris, Colin.

Burke, E. (1905), *Reflections on the French Revolution*, London, Methuen.

Club Jean Moulin (1968), *Les Citoyens au pouvoir: 12 régions, 2000 communes*, Paris, Le Seuil.

Dayries, J.-J. and M. Dayries (1978), *La Régionalisation*, Paris, PUF.

Drevet, J.-F. (1988), *1992-2000: les régions françaises entre l'Europe et le déclin*, Paris, Souffles.

Fourastié, J. (1979), *Les trente glorieuses: ou la révolution invisible de 1946 à 1975*, Paris, Fayard.

Gravier, J. F. (1947), *Paris et le désert français*, Paris, Portulan.

—— (1970), *La Question régionale*, Paris, Flammarion.

Gruber, A. (1986), *La Décentralisation et les institutions administratives*, Paris, Colin.

Lafont, R. (1967), *La Révolution régionaliste*, Paris, Gallimard.

—— (1971), *Décoloniser en France*, Paris, Gallimard.

Lanversin, J. de, A. Lanza and F. Zitouni (1989), *La Région et l'Aménagement du territoire dans la décentralisation*, 4th. edition, Paris, Economica.

Lévy, M. L. (1982), *La Population de la France des années 80*, Paris, Hatier.

Mény, Y. (1974), *Centralisation et décentralisation dans le débat politique français (1945-1969)*, Paris, Pichon and Durand-Auzias.

Merriman, J. M. (ed.) (1982), *French Cities in the Nineteenth Century*, London, Hutchinson.

Perrineau, P. (1987), *Régions: le baptême des urnes*, Paris, Pedone.

Pisani, E. (1969), *La Région... pour quoi faire? ou le triomphe des jacondins*, Paris, Calmann Lévy.

Schmidt, V. A. (1990), *Democratizing France: the political and administrative history of decentralization*, Cambridge, CUP.

Uhrich, R. (1987), *La France inverse: les régions en mutation*, Paris, Economica.

Weber, E. (1977), *Peasants into Frenchmen: the modernization of rural France 1870-1914*, London, Chatto and Windus.

Zeldin, T. (1977), *France 1848-1945*, Oxford, OUP.

NETHERLANDS

GERMANY

Ostend

Antwerp
ANTWERP

WEST-
FLANDERS

Gent

EAST-
FLANDERS

LIMBURG

Brussels
BRABANT

HAINAUT

Liège

LIEGE

German speaking region

Charleroi

Namur

BELGIUM

FRANCE

NAMUR

LUXEMBOURG

LUXEMBOURG

0   50   100

kilometres

Regionalism in Belgium
Peter Wagstaff

1. Introduction

'There is a comparison to Belgium within Europe: Czechoslovakia, the nation
that split in two at the end of 1992. Animosity between the two Belgian factions
appears far worse than that between Czechs and Slovaks. And culturally they
have much less in common than the Slovak tribes, one being Germanic, the
other Latin' (*The European*, 1-4 July 1993, p. 8).

The comparison of Belgium with what was, until recently, Czechoslovakia,
appears striking, even bizarre. It is nonetheless one that has been made as the
spotlight falls temporarily on Belgium's presidency of the European Community
in the second half of 1993. An explanation of the comparison is not hard to find,
even if the underlying reasons which prompted it do not bear close scrutiny. It
can be argued that, to a far greater extent than any neighbouring country, the
Belgian state was an artificial creation, accommodating the desires and interests
of the Great Powers following the revolution of 1830. Statehood and nationhood
were not, therefore, co-terminous, despite the best intentions and efforts of the
ruling élites to awaken a sense of national unity. Throughout its modern history,
then, there has been an ever-present threat of fracture or rift between the various
elements that make up Belgium. The nature of these elements, and of the rifts
which threaten them, is not as clear-cut as might be suggested by a superficial
familiarity with a state apparently sandwiched between, and polarised by, the
Netherlands to the North and France to the South. The relationship between
two linguistic communities - the Walloons and the Flemings (French and Dutch-
speaking) - is of course a major and constant feature of debate, but it represents
only one of a number of significant faultlines in Belgian national life, any of
which could, and from time to time do, call into question the unitary nature of
the state. Indeed, there seems to be a semi-official recognition that Belgium's
natural condition is one of change, 'the gradual but unavoidable transformation
of a strictly centralised State entity into a regional or federal State system'
(Senelle, 1987, p. 8).

The stresses acting upon the Belgian state are political, cultural, and
economic; their complex inter-dependence and often conflicting effects reveal
unusual aspects of national institutional change. Unusual in that Belgium, which
for most of its formal existence as a state had conformed to the dictates of
unified nationhood, has in recent decades made substantial moves in the
direction of a sort of regional federalism not unlike that which characterised the
territory before the state was created. Unusual, too, in that the cultural factors
make themselves felt in the particularly acute form of a linguistic division which
reveals not only fears of domination by one language group over another, but
also a reversal of dominant roles brought about by economic circumstances. The
analysis of this 'gradual but unavoidable transformation' will begin with an
examination of the historical and cultural features which have set Belgium on its
present course. This will be followed by a survey of economic factors which have
transformed the relationship between the two main constituencies in Belgian life
and, therefore, the political landscape. Finally, I shall address the question of the
succession of political and constitutional settlements which, over the last quarter

EUROPA 1(2/3) 1994 39-50 © Intellect Ltd 1994

of a century, have been put forward in response to the increasingly deep schisms in Belgian society.

2. Two communities: historical and cultural feature

The geographical and physical limits of a Belgian state are not obvious. 'Natural' frontiers, such as the river Scheldt in the north, or the Ardennes-Eifel hills in the south, do not, on the whole, coincide with the political boundaries, while in the north-west the plains of Flanders merge imperceptibly with those of northern France. It is, therefore, hardly surprising that external commentators on the origins of Belgium generally concur with the view that the country was 'an artificial creation of the great powers' (Fitzmaurice, 1984, p. 418), 'the most contrived country in western Europe' (Huggett, 1969, p. 1). From its origins in the aftermath of the Congress of Vienna, the new state was seen as 'a bulwark against France [...] a fortress on France's northern border' (Kossmann-Putto, 1987, p. 40). Sources closer to the Belgian State, however, view the matter differently, while pre-empting the sort of observations outlined above: 'Abroad the question often arises whether Belgium is not an artificial State which owes its existence to the striving for political and military equilibrium on the part of France, Great Britain, Prussia and the Danubian Monarchy.

Nothing could be further from the truth [...] The North and South Low Countries (i.e. the present-day Kingdom of the Netherlands and the present-day Kingdom of Belgium) formed a political entity, created during the 15th and 16th centuries, which consisted of various principalities and had, through the genius of the Dukes of Burgundy, been made into a particularly prosperous economic and political unit' (Senelle, 1987, p. 7).

These comments are representative of many attempts to construct an a posteriori normality and legitimacy for the fledgling state as a nation united in its origins and its aspirations. The influences on Belgian origins are, however, legion. Split between French and Germanic influence (west and east of the Scheldt river) at the Treaty of Verdun in 843, the territory witnessed the rise of the duchy of Brabant and of the counties of Flanders and Hainaut in feudal times. Its period of greatest cultural dominance came with the rule of the Dukes of Burgundy in the fourteenth and fifteenth centuries. The Low Countries as a whole were allied by royal marriage with the Hapsburg empire at the end of the fifteenth century. Hapsburg domination lasted for a further hundred years, when the seven northern provinces, under the title of the 'United Provinces', gained independent status, and the southern provinces passed under Spanish dominion. A century and a half of intermittent strife, in which France was a major actor, led to the Treaty of Aix-la-Chapelle in 1748, when the territory of Belgium passed into Austrian hands. Further conflict led to French invasion and, finally annexation. From 1795 until 1815 French control imposed a governing élite, the impact of whose presence would be felt for generations. The allocation of the territory to the Kingdom of the Netherlands at the Congress of Vienna in 1815 was followed by a period of intense religious and political struggle leading to the revolution against the regime of William I in 1830 and the subsequent formation of the Belgian state with the drafting of a Constitution in 1831. No unitary state had existed on this territory prior to this date. Indeed, it might be argued that what preceded it was a loose, quasi-federalist grouping of provinces enjoying a considerable measure of autonomy under successive regimes (Logie, 1980).

The settlement of 1831 embodied the resolution of territorial antagonisms implicit in the successive periods of French and Dutch control. Thus in the space of not much more than one generation, between 1795 and 1831, the foundations for the modern Belgian state were laid. At the same time, however, the main elements of tension and conflict were being incorporated into the structure. The arrival of the French armies in 1792, heralding annexation three years later, led to the imposition of a jacobine centralisation which was to survive the fifteen year period of Dutch rule from 1815. Liberal and Catholic opinion combined to produce sufficient anti-Orangist and anti-Protestant feeling to oust the Dutch in the revolution of 1830, and the Constitution of 1831 enshrined the principle of a constitutional monarchy at the head of a unitary state with a parliamentary system of government. Even in the first flush of statehood, however, the fissiparous tendencies of the new Belgium were noted by a contemporary historian: 'En Belgique, il y a des partis et des provinces, et point de nation. Comme une tente dressée pour une nuit, la monarchie nouvelle, après nous avoir abrités contre la tempête, disparaîtra sans laisser de traces' ('In Belgium, there are parties and provinces, but no nation. Like a tent set up for one night, the new monarchy, after sheltering us from the storm, will disappear without trace' (Nothomb (1834), in Hasquin, 1982, p. 22). The inaccuracy of that prediction does not negate the underlying implication that some form of conflict or opposition was the most likely condition of the new state.

The imposition of a unitary, centralised structure was matched by a policy of unilingualism in all but name which took no account of the existence of two juxtaposed linguistic groups. While the majority of the population was Dutch-speaking, located in the Flanders provinces in the north of the country, the newly-created state was, to all intents and purposes, francophone, with its legacy of bourgeois French-speaking élites and a governmental and administrative structure on the French model. The Constitution offered, in theory at least, freedom in language use, but laws and decrees were all promulgated in French and, although 'Flemish' translations existed, only the French texts had legal validity. This unilingual reality was not, however, a main source of discord in the early years. It was only as the nineteenth century progressed that traditional cleavages on religious and social grounds were replaced by division along linguistic lines (Wils, 1993).

Control of the newly-constituted Belgium lay with a political class dominated by the traditional opposition of Catholics and Liberals, who alternated in power for much of the nineteenth century. The predominance of the French-speaking sector of the population was compounded, for at least half a century after independence, by an electoral system based on property qualification: by and large it was the francophone bourgeois élites who participated in the electoral process. In 1846 Belgium contained 2.5 million Dutch speakers, 1.8 million French speakers, and a mere 45,000 qualified electors. The exclusion of almost the entirety of the Flemish population was compounded by the effects of demographic changes evident as early as the late nineteenth century and persisting up to the present day. The Walloon population, as a proportion of the whole, reached a peak in the 1880s, when the success of the industrial revolution in the southern coalfield, combined with the progressive impoverishment of the economy of Flanders, led to southward migration. From then on, however, the balance started to alter, in terms of both demographic trends and cultural and linguistic assertiveness. Partial reform of the constitution in 1892-93 initiated a process of extension of voting rights to all adult males by 1920-21 (universal male and female suffrage for national elections was not obtained until 1948).

In parallel with these political developments, which tended towards an enfranchisement of the numerically dominant but politically impotent Flemings, changes in the status of the two language groups were gradually introduced. These culminated in the major reform of 1898 guaranteeing equal status for Dutch and French at national level. The movement, then, was away from a French unilingualism applied indifferently throughout the country, and towards a limited bilingualism. However, the apparently simple demarcation between unilingual and bilingual groupings masks a number of complex issues. While it had long been clear that the Dutch-speaking community occupied the northern half of the country and French-speakers occupied the southern half (with a small community of German speakers in the east), no attempt had been made formally to delineate these two areas in precise geographical terms.

The de facto existence of a francophone community bordering France in the south, and of a Dutch-speaking community in the north, bordering Holland, received official sanction only in the mid-1960s, since when linguistic divisions have been clearly marked on the administrative map of Belgium. The complexity of allegiance is revealed in the status of Brussels, posing an additional difficulty, and one which has proved perhaps the most intractable throughout this entire debate for, while the capital is situated in Flemish territory, the language of its governing élites is French. Further, the growth in the city's population, and the consequent encroachment of largely francophone migrants on surrounding communities has led to tension and, ultimately, to the status of a separate region with its own complex and evolving linguistic identity (Witte *et al*, 1984).

The designation of two unilingual regions for the country as a whole, separated by an official language line, dates from 1932, although formal legal status was only afforded in 1963, and consolidated by further legislation in 1970 in an attempt to deal with the anomalous situation of Brussels. As a result of this legislation, there is now formal definition of the linguistic regions. The Dutch-speaking region comprises the Provinces of West Flanders, East Flanders, Antwerp, and Limburg, together with the districts of Louvain and Hal-Vilvorde which are part of the Province of Brabant (i.e. the northern part of the country). The French-speaking region comprises the Provinces of Hainaut, Namur, Luxembourg, and Liège (except the eastern part) and the district of Nivelles which is part of the Province of Brabant (i.e. the southern part of the country). The German-speaking region comprises the eastern part of the Province of Liège. The bilingual region of Greater Brussels comprises the 19 *communes* of the urban area of which the capital is a part (Senelle, 1987, p. 10). The relationship between these various regions, and their current status in terms of political and administrative responsibility, will be examined in greater detail in the third section below. The measures outlined reflect an acknowledgement of the cultural and linguistic reality concealed behind the image of the unitary state, and of the inevitable abandonment of the ambition for a nationwide bilingualism that would successfully mask the divisions.

There have been few occasions in the history of Belgium when the cohesiveness of the state has seemed attainable. Most obviously, perhaps, the wars of 1914-18 and 1939-45 might be seen as a rallying-point for national unity in the face of aggression or the violation of neutrality. And yet it was the resentment of the (largely Flemish) foot soldiers against their francophone officer corps in the trenches of the First World War that gave a boost to the Flemish movement. A generation later the early release of Flemish, but not Walloon, prisoners of war by the Germans, and the ambiguous, possibly collaborationist stance of the King, Leopold III, led to equally strong resentment in the French-speaking community, culminating in the strike of 1950 in protest against the King's return, and his forced abdication in favour of his son, Baudouin (Aron, 1977).

The political forces which have dominated Belgian life since the nineteenth century fall broadly into three categories: Social Christians (of Catholic origin), Liberals, and Socialists. All three were unitary in origin, each having a single structure for the entire country. The modifications to the Constitution in 1892-3 and 1918-19 which brought about the establishment of universal suffrage, accommodated the continuation of political division on religious and social lines until well after the Second World War. The Catholic Party became the *Parti Social Chrétien* (PSC) in 1945 and occupied one side of the political divide. The anti-clerical vote was split on a class basis between the old-established Liberal Party (founded in 1846), which became the *Parti de la Liberté et du Progrès* (PLP) in 1961, and the Socialist *Parti Socialiste Belge* (PSB), dating from 1885 (Senelle, 1965, p. 43). For the first half of the twentieth century and beyond, the domination of the political scene by these three traditional parties was almost total. Between the end of the First World War and the early 1960s, when the language conflict took a sharper turn, the Social Christians, the Liberals, and the PSB took, on average, more than 88% of the parliamentary vote, and were in fact the only parties to participate in government, with the brief exception of the Communist Party for eight months immediately after the Second World War (Mughan, 1983, p. 437). The growth of parties representing the interests of one or other linguistic community, mostly in the years following the Second World War, led the three main parties to split along similar lines, reflecting the Flemish-Walloon division. As a result, cross-party regional solidarity is probably as strongly delineated as the national political cleavages. The laws of 1962-3 which traced the demarcation line between linguistic regions were intended to defuse the political element of the linguistic dispute. The gains in that direction were short-lived, however, since animosity between communities escalated continually until, in March 1968, the government was brought down by the controversy surrounding the proposed transfer of the French-speaking section of the University of Louvain to Walloon territory. The Social Christian Party subsequently relinquished its unitarian stance, splitting into two to become the PSC (of French expression) and the *Christelijke Volkspartij* (of Dutch expression). This scission was prompted, in part at least, by the arrival on the scene of a number of *communautaire* parties (i.e. those dedicated to the interests of specific linguistic groups). Throughout the post-war period, the tide of nationalism - particularly Flemish - led to the formation of such parties. The *Volksunie* movement was founded in 1948, followed shortly thereafter, in predictable counter-reaction, by the *Front Démocratique des Francophones* (FDF) and by the *Rassemblement Wallon* (RW).

The balance of power within Belgium, then, has shifted substantially in recent generations. The Flemish population, always numerically superior and increasingly dominant in economic terms, has gradually come into its own, undermining the hegemony of the influential French-speaking minority. This prompted at first an attempt to legislate for an officially bilingual country and subsequently the recognition of the reality of two distinct linguistic communities evolving along separate if parallel lines. The result has been that the concept of the unitary state, and of a notional bilingualism within it, has been under severe and sustained pressure. Throughout the entire period of Belgian statehood, the political and cultural forces outlined above have been sustained and given direction by a range of complex and often conflicting economic pressures.

3. Two communities: economic factors

The nineteenth-century industrial revolution, based on coal, began earlier in Belgium than elsewhere in continental Europe. Exploitation of the massive Borinage coalfield which ran from the French border through Mons, Charleroi and Namur to Liège and beyond - in Walloon territory along the Sambre-Meuse valley - gave Belgium a faster rate of industrial growth during the mid-century than either Great Britain or Germany. While the coal and iron ore deposits in the southern, francophone, part of the country at first ensured a thriving economic base, the Dutch-speaking North was for a long time unable to match this achievement. The Walloon region retained its dominant position in the Belgian national economy well into the twentieth century although, as a proportion of the country's industrial workforce, the Walloon population had started to decline by the 1880s. This can be partly explained by a natural process of industrial and technological development. The primary activities of coal and ore extraction, together with basic iron and steel production, were slowly complemented by the next stage of industrial development, with the production of non-ferrous metals and chemicals in the coastal zone around Antwerp in the Flemish north. Exploitation of the mineral resources of Belgium's Congo colony also tended to concentrate activity in the privileged ports and their hinterland. This meant growth and the beginnings of prosperity for Flanders, which boasts the Belgian coastline in its entirety (a mere 65 kilometres). By the early years of the twentieth century, Flemish industrial production was rising (admittedly from a very low base) more rapidly than Walloon production, which itself reached a peak around 1930. From that point onwards, the Brussels-Antwerp axis was the focus for dynamic growth in industrial sectors such as vehicles and petrochemicals, flourishing into the 1950s and beyond. In later years, the difficulties experienced by traditional heavy industry, such as cheap imports and falling demand for coal and steel, affected the Walloon Sambre-Meuse coalfield even more seriously than the neighbouring Nord-Pas de Calais of northern France, and by 1982 the Walloon share of the Belgian industrial workforce had fallen to 27.7% (Thomas, 1990, p. 38). By contrast, the gradual build up of manufacturing activity in Flanders brought with it a growth in regional self-confidence and, in its train, an assertion of the rights of the Dutch-speaking population.

It should be noted that it is industry and commerce which have been the motors of the Belgian economy. The role of agriculture, for so long a dominant activity in France, for example, is tiny: less than 5% of the active population is engaged in farming, and its contribution to the economy has fallen steadily, from 6.5% of GDP in 1960 to 1.8% in 1990 (*L'Etat de l'Europe*, 1992, p. 510).

Demographic trends only served to reinforce the shift of influence from North to South: the population of Wallonia has remained stagnant while the birthrate of the Flemish areas has risen substantially throughout the twentieth century. In the period from 1920 to 1982, the Walloon population grew by a mere 350,000, while the Flemish population increased by 1.91 million (Thomas,

1990, p. 41). As population growth is translated into the distribution of parliamentary seats, the growth in Flemish influence is a natural concomitant of a rising birthrate. Most importantly, it is in the active population that the shifts are most clearly revealed. Between 1947 and 1961, there was an increase in the proportion of the active population in all the northern provinces except East Flanders, whereas all the provinces of Wallonia, without exception, suffered a decline (Huggett, 1969, p. 83). It is hardly surprising, therefore, that political divisions are also highlighted and modified by these demographic changes. The Catholic-based PSC traditionally draws substantial support from the Flemish population; its influence has therefore been consolidated by Flemish ascendancy. If Flanders is predominantly Catholic, then Wallonia has a more secular culture, providing support for the PSB and the small Belgian Communist Party, as well as the PLP. As well as marking one more division between the communities, this religious/anti-clerical opposition is a reflection of the industrial climate as it has developed over the years. Belgium as a whole has one of the highest population densities in Europe, with over 250 inhabitants per square kilometre and, while it is Antwerp, Ghent and Brussels which are the most crowded areas now, during the early period of Walloon industrial ascendancy in the second half of the nineteenth century the population was highly concentrated in the south. This concentration provided vast reserves of cheap labour, a situation which accounts for Marx's description of Belgium as 'a capitalist's paradise' (Huggett, 1969, p. 28), but also explains the appeal of the anti-clerical parties of the left, notably the PSB. Labour militancy in the Walloon coalfield, leading to strikes and production stoppages, has not been reflected in the Flemish north, where the Catholic church has normally been quick to condemn militant action and where industrial peace has therefore tended to reign. These factors explain, in part at least, the lack of investment in the stagnant Walloon industrial economy, and the relative success of Flanders in attracting incoming investment in industry. The post-war period, and particularly the 1960s, saw, therefore, a rapid growth in the economy of Flanders, in terms of manufacturing industry and the service sector. The change in the relative importance of the industrial and service sectors in the period 1960-1990 is instructive: a gradual decline in industry's contribution from 40.9% of GDP in 1960 to 30.1% in 1990 has been mirrored by a rise in service sector activity from 52.6% to 68.1%.

Brussels especially became a centre for service sector employment, enjoying a period of enormous expansion in this area from the late 1950s onwards. The obvious stimulus was the creation of the European Economic Community and the selection of Brussels as the seat of the Commission and the Council of Ministers. The magnetic effect on foreign companies and countries alike was striking, with the establishment of more than two hundred embassies and the offices of over eleven hundred international organisations (Thomas, 1990, p. 39). The very success of Brussels as a focus for service sector activity has, however, contributed to serious problems elsewhere, particularly in Wallonia, which lacks the range of provincial urban development to compete with the capital. In comparison with Flemish territory, with its long-established urban tradition rooted in the Middle Ages (Bruges, Leuwen), Wallonia's urban development is based essentially on the industrial expansion of the nineteenth century, and its towns consequently tend to lack the facilities which would permit diversification and growth.

In the modern period, therefore, three factors combine to produce a need for radical change to the institutional framework of the Belgian state. First, the growth in the confidence and economic power of the Flemish area, to match its demographic ascendancy. Second, the concomitant weakness of the Walloon constituency, and its failure to manage successfully its reconversion from a heavy industrial past. Third, the status of Brussels and its surrounding area: economically buoyant through an explosion in tertiary activity, yet occupying an ambiguous position both culturally and linguistically. Brussels of course is not the only part of Belgium to present an anomalous and potentially conflictual situation. At various points along the dividing line that separates the Flemish and French-speaking regions, arrangements have had to be made to protect the interests of linguistic minorities from either side, with similar arrangements in place for the benefit of minority German-speakers in those areas adjacent to the Germanophone zones in the east. Of particular note is the situation of the enclave known as the Fourons, on the northern fringe of the French-speaking province of Liège. Responsibility for the district was transferred in 1963 to the Flemish province of Limburg, provoking dissatisfaction and resentment which provided fertile ground for French and Flemish nationalists, leading to a bitter dispute and the downfall of the centre-right government in 1987 (Poole, 1987).

It was these factors, and the growing acerbity of relations between the various parties concerned, that led to the succession of revisions to the Belgian constitution from the 1960s onwards.

4. Constitutional revision: towards a federal structure

The signs of Flemish–Walloon dissension were sufficiently evident in the years following the Second World War to prompt the setting up of a research centre, the Centre Harmel, in the search for *'la solution nationale des problèmes sociaux, politiques et juridiques en régions wallonne et flamande'* ('a national solution to social, political and juridical problems in the Walloon and Flemish regions') (Supplément au *Soir*, 15 December 1992). This ensured that informed and influential debate on the subject, and agreement on reform measures, were carried on in an extra-parliamentary forum in the years that followed, with the Parliament exercising an a posteriori legislative role. The deliberations of the Centre Harmel took account, throughout the 1950s, of both the growth in Flemish economic power and influence and, in response, a gradually increasing determination on the part of the Walloon community to protect its declining interests by pressing for a more federalist state structure. The Walloon population found such a structure all the more attractive as it watched the Flemish parliamentary majority direct state investment towards the Flemish economy. By the end of the 1950s, the Centre Harmel had proposed that the two language communities should be granted cultural autonomy, and the linguistic laws of 1962-63 enshrined this principle. In addition, these laws brought an entirely new element into play by sanctioning an equivalence between cultural and territorial divisions. The linguistic dividing line between Flemish and French-speaking territories henceforth appears on the map as a physical feature.

In the three decades that have followed this early, important recognition of a match between linguistic and geographical divisions, further constitutional revisions have been made in response to a complicated interplay of political demands and compromises. The 1970 revision saw the introduction of two new concepts which were intended to meet the differing demands of the two major language groups. In response to Flemish requests, the principle of the

Communauté emerged. This represents an entity formed according to cultural (i.e. linguistic) criteria. At the same time, and in response to Walloon desires for an element of socio-economic autonomy, the principle of the territorially-based *Région* was brought into being. At once, each of the three *Communautés* (French, Flemish, and German-speaking) assumed responsibility for cultural and linguistic affairs. The development of a framework for the operation of the *Régions* was, however, a much more complex matter, since it proved impossible in the early stages to resolve the question of Brussels, with its superimposed language communities. A further revision of the Constitution in 1980 merely extended the responsibilities of the *Communautés* in areas such as health care, while at the same time giving a theoretically autonomous status to the French and Flemish *Régions* (Mabille, 1986). By the revision of 1988, however, a much wider range of responsibilities was devolved to *Communautés* (in particular education) and *Régions* (public works and transport). By this stage, something like 30% of the national budget was allocated at the level of *Communauté* and *Région*, although this substantial budgetary responsibility was not yet matched by an equivalent democratic responsibility: regional and *communauté* councils were not directly elected. Perhaps the most significant advance lay in the fact that the Brussels region was defined, at least provisionally, within the limits of its 19 *communes*.

A notable feature of the constitutional revisions which have taken place over the last quarter century has been the increasing momentum of change. The process has been a gradual but ineluctable movement in the direction of a federal state, and the most recent revision of the constitution, debated at the end of 1992 and passed into law on 14 July 1993, has been hailed as the necessary, decisive, and perhaps final step towards federalism. There is an unfortunate irony in the fact that this watershed legislation was closely followed by the death of Baudouin, *roi des Belges* and institutional symbol of the attempts to forge and to maintain a united kingdom. The implications of the 1993 revision are far-reaching, although in some respects perhaps not quite as far-reaching as the proponents of a fully-fledged federalism would wish. The status of the three *Régions* (Wallonia, Flanders, and Brussels-Capital) has been confirmed and consolidated, with a range of responsibilities specified. Regional development, transport and public works, housing, economic and employment policy, environmental matters, and relations with the *communes* and *provinces*, all depend on decision-making at regional level. By the same token, the responsibilities of the three *Communautés* (French, Flemish, and German-speaking), have been specified, and relate largely to the cultural sphere. Cultural heritage, radio and television, tourism, policy for youth, education, inter-*communauté* cooperation, health and family policy, form the bulk of *Communauté* responsibilities, together with the question of language use in administration and education. The major problem for the *Communautés* has been, and remains, the division of responsibilities within the Brussels-Capital region itself which, with its two-language mix, fits uneasily into the *Communauté* framework. Resolution of the problem depends on the success of a complicated set of institutions designed to ensure even-handedness while acknowledging the specific identities of the two language communities, which must co-exist on the same territory. Regional matters are dealt with, as for the two other *Régions*, by a directly-elected regional council, while community matters are subject to a complex tri-partite regime composed of commissions for French, Flemish, and joint responsibilities. However, the most radical element in the 1993 revision concerns the alterations to Belgium's bi-cameral parliamentary system. The effect of these changes is to bring to an end the previous equality of power between the Senate and the *Chambre des Représentants*. Henceforth, the *Chambre* has wide-ranging decision-making powers, in the realm of the budget, ministerial responsibilities, motions of confidence, which it can exercise without regard to the Senate. True, certain areas continue to require joint *Chambre*-Senate agreement, such as constitutional revisions, international treaties, and the delegation of powers to the EC and other international bodies. The role of the Senate, on the other hand, becomes more generally consultative, with the power to propose legislation, to which the *Chambre* can react as it thinks fit. The composition of the Senate is, at least in part, indicative of its role as a federal chamber. The current number of 184 senators is reduced to 71, 40 of whom (25 Dutch, 15 French-speaking) will be directly elected. A further 21 (10 Dutch, 10 French, 1 German-speaking) will be nominated by the three *conseils de communauté*, with another 10 (6 Dutch and 4 French-speaking) co-opted by the previous category. Thus, 31 senators will derive their status from the *Communautés*, reflecting the federal intentions of the newly-constituted senate. Overall, however, the ratio of Dutch- to French-speaking senators (41 to 29, or 58.6% to 41.4%) is very closely linked to the ratio of the two groups within the population as a whole. Paradoxically, this does not reflect the normal mode of representation in an institution structured on federal lines. The expectation is of a system based either on equal representation for the constituent parts (e.g. the U.S Senate) or one in which the smaller constituencies receive compensatory representation (e.g. the German *Bundesrat*). There is one further feature of the newly revised constitutional arrangements which tends to belie the federalist intentions. Unlike most federal states, Belgium retains a judicial system which, in terms of its organisation and its day-to-day working, is common to the state as a whole, rather than being allowed to evolve separately within the *Communautés*.

5. Conclusion

It would seem, therefore, that Belgium has perhaps not advanced quite as far down the road towards the federal state, even with the most recent constitutional revision, as commentators have claimed. Nonetheless, many features of federalism are in place, and it is clear that their introduction is seen as a bulwark against the quasi-separatist tendencies of the two major language communities. In addition, difficult economic circumstances since the end of the 1980s have seen a concomitant rise in the threat of political extremism: in Antwerp, the three traditional parties, Liberals, Social-Christians, Socialists, together received less than 50% of the votes at the 1991 election, to the benefit of - chiefly - the extreme right Vlaams Blok with over 25%. In this context, too, federalism is felt to offer an alternative to sharply focused antagonisms. At the same time as the institutional structure of the Belgian state has been subject to these changes, successive governments, whether of the centre-left under M. Martens between 1988 and 1991, or of the centre-right under M. Dehaene since 1991, have sought to promote the status of Brussels as European capital, rather than simply as the home of the European Commission and bridgehead for countless international organisations and companies. It is ironic that Belgium should be called upon to promote harmonious relationships among the twelve member states during its presidency of the EC in the second half of 1993, when it is struggling to achieve a tenuous harmony between conflicting communities at home. Provisions in the Maastricht Treaty for regional and community executives to be represented, at some future date, at the Council of Ministers, are seen as a means of defusing regional antagonisms by allowing them to be expressed in a wider, supra-national forum. A Belgium which aspires to a form of federalism within a Europe where similar aspirations are being voiced, however tentatively, is one which acknowledges the existence of the faultline between Europe's Latin and Germanic cultures within its own borders and yet hopes for a reconciliation of its own conflicts on a wider stage.

It will be clear from the above that, given the uniquely dominant influence of the language question on Belgian national life, there are few conclusions to be drawn that are directly applicable to the regional debate within the EU as a whole. Indeed, even within Belgium itself, the nine pre-existing regional units have been largely eclipsed by the major three-way division (four Dutch-speaking, four French-speaking, and Brussels-Capital with its own complex formulation). However, the impact over the long term of the strengthening of strictly regional representation at various levels of EU deliberations, whether at the Council of Ministers or the Committee of the Regions, may well encourage the emergence of a more measured, and less politically charged, atmosphere than has been evident in recent months and years.

References

Aron, R. (1977), *Léopold III ou le choix impossible: février 1934 - juillet 1940*, Paris, Plon.

Feron, F. and A. Thoraval (eds.) (1992), *L'Etat de l'Europe*, Paris, La Découverte.

Fitzmaurice, J. (1984), 'Belgium: Reluctant Federalism', *Parliamentary Affairs*, 37, pp. 418-433.

Frognier, A. P., M. Quevit and M. Stenbock (1982), 'Regional Imbalances and Centre-Periphery Relations in Belgium', in Rokkan, S. and D. W. Urwin (eds.) (1982), *The Politics of Territorial Identity: Studies in European Regionalism*, London, Sage.

Hasquin, H. (1982), *Historiographie et politique: Essai sur l'histoire de la Belgique et la Wallonie* (2nd edition), Charleroi, Institut Jules Destrée.

Huggett, F. E. (1969), *Modern Belgium*, London, Pall Mall Press.

Kossmann-Putto, J. A. and E. H. Kossmann (1987), *The Low Countries: History of the Northern and Southern Netherlands*, Flanders, Flemish Netherlands Foundation.

Logie, J. (1980), *1830: De la régionalisation à l'indépendance*, Paris, Duculot.

Mabille, X. (1986), *Histoire politique de la Belgique: facteurs et acteurs de changement*, Brussels, Centre de recherche et d'information socio-politiques.

Mughan, A. (1983), 'Accommodation or Diffusion in the Management of Linguistic Conflict in Belgium', *Political Studies* (1983), XXXI, pp. 434-451.

Poole, A. (1987), 'The Fourons: a microcosm of Belgium's linguistic problems', *The Linguist*, 26 (2), pp. 52-56.

Senelle, R. (1987), *The Reform of the Belgian State*, Vol. IV, Brussels, Ministry of Foreign Affairs and External Trade (Memo from Belgium No. 196).

Thomas, P. (1990), 'Belgium's North-South Divide and the Walloon Regional Problem', *Geography*, No. 326, Vol. 75, Part I (January 1990), pp. 36-50.

Wils, L. (1993), 'Belgium on the Path to Equal Language Rights up to 1939', in *Ethnic Groups and Language Rights (Comparative Studies on Governments and Non-Dominant Ethnic Groups in Europe, 1850-1940*, Vol. III), Dartmouth, New York University Press.

Witte, E. *et al* (1984), *Le Bilinguisme en Belgique: le cas de Bruxelles*, Brussels, Editions de l'Université de Bruxelles.

Federalism in Germany
Theo Stammen

1. Introduction

When the Federal Republic of Germany (*die Bundesrepublik*) was founded in 1949, its political and institutional order included a large federalist component. Three factors contributed to this. The first stemmed from the reality of the situation at the time: most of the federal states (*Länder*) in the *Bundesrepublik* had been either freshly created or set up along existing lines by the Allied Occupying Powers in the period between 1946 and 1949 and were consequently older than the *Bundesrepublik* itself. The second factor can be traced to the normative status of the 'Frankfurt Documents', which the three western military governors imposed on the German Prime Minister (*Ministerpräsident*) in the summer of 1948 as the framework for the creation of the West German Constitution, or Basic Law (*Grundgesetz*), and which stipulated that the new German constitutional order should be democratic and federalist. Finally, a third, traditional, factor came into play: in contrast to the majority of centrally-organised European nation-states, such as France or Great Britain, Germany had, throughout its recent history, always had a federalist order in keeping with its great regional variety. In the nineteenth and twentieth centuries, different forms of federalist system had alternated: either confederative (*Deutscher Bund*) or federal (*Deutsches Reich*) bringing together principalities and dukedoms. The Weimar Republic, too, was a federalist state, which established a precarious balance of power between central power and regions, *Reich* and *Länder*, with the balance tilted in favour of the *Reich*. It was notable, also, that the National Socialist dictatorship very quickly got rid of the *Länder*, and with them the principle of a federalist structure, so as to consolidate the centralist power structure of the NS system.

Federalism, then, along with the principles of the rule of law, democracy, republicanism and the social state, took its place as a fundamental feature of the *Bundesrepublik's* new constitutional order. It is a principle which has consistently underpinned the structure of this political system, but which has nonetheless been subject to considerable change in the period since 1949.

It is worth noting, too, that the second German state to be founded in 1949, the German Democratic Republic (DDR), was a federative state, according to its first constitution which was very much in the image of the Weimar constitution, with five *Länder* and a parliamentary chamber *(Reichskammer)*. By the beginning of the 1950s, this original federative component of the DDR constitution was abolished in favour of a strict centralisation of state power linked to the construction of socialism. Fourteen administrative districts ((*Verwaltungs*)-*Bezirke*) took the place of the *Länder*, and the *Landeskammer* ceased to exist as a DDR institution. Interestingly, in 1990, during the process of German unification, the re-formation of the five *Länder* in the DDR (as it still was at the time) echoed this tradition. In October 1990, these five *Länder* formally joined the Federal Republic on the basis of the unification agreement and Article 23 of the *Grundgesetz*. The number of *Länder* was thus increased from eleven to sixteen.

It is this federalist structure of the *Bundesrepublik*, at present still the only traditionally federalist member state of the European Community, which is the

EUROPA 1(2/3) 1994 51-67 © Intellect Ltd 1994

subject of this chapter. Above all, it is the following three problem areas which need to be addressed and analysed:

1. The formation and development of the federative order of the *Bundesrepublik*;
2. The constitutional significance of federalism, and
3. The current political significance of German federalism in relation to reunification and European integration.

2. The Federal State System in Germany

1. The basic principles of the *Grundgesetz* are set out in Article 20: 'The Federal Republic of Germany is a democratic and social federal state.' This, in conjunction with Article 28, which states that 'constitutional law in the *Länder* must comply with the principles of the republican, democratic, and social state under the rule of law in accordance with the *Grundgesetz*', contains the normative basis for the *Bundesrepublik's* constitutional order. The basic meaning of these five structural principles is essentially underlined in Article 79, paragraph 3 of the *Grundgesetz*, which expressly excludes any alteration to these constitutional rules ('Any alteration to this *Grundgesetz* which affects the division of the federal state into *Länder*, the fundamental involvement of the *Länder* with the legislative process, or the principles set down in Articles 1 and 20, is inadmissible'). This means that not even a 100% majority in the national parliament (*Bundestag*) and the representative chamber for the *Länder* (*Bundesrat*) would be able to remove the federative structure of the *Bundesrepublik* by the legitimate process of a constitutional amendment; accordingly, there has been talk of an 'eternal guarantee' of federalism. Although it is always problematical in political life to talk of 'eternity', this formula makes it expressly clear that federalism is especially protected and guaranteed as a structuring principle of the *Bundesrepublik's* political and institutional order: it belongs to the permanent core of German constitutional law, the existence of which cannot be infringed in the context of European integration.

2. The principle of federalism (Article 20 of the *Grundgesetz*) determines the vertical structure of the political system, If, as seems appropriate, we include local government, then the overall political structure of the *Bundesrepublik* can be visualised in terms of a large building with three separate but linked storeys consisting first, on the ground floor, of local government, with its municipalities (*Gemeinde*), towns (*Städte*) and districts (*Kreisen*) then, on the first floor, of the sixteen *Länder* each with its own constitution and political institutions, and finally, on the upper floor, of the federal state with its central state organs. The *Grundgesetz* as the constitution of the *Bundesrepublik* determines the complex architectonics of the entire building. This piece of architecture could be extended to include a fourth floor if the European Community were included, as may perhaps be appropriate in the future with the realisation of European union. The political activity that takes place simultaneously on all floors is correspondingly diverse: each level has its own political tasks and responsibilities, its own processes for the development of informed political opinion and decision-making, with appropriate political institutions which are democratically constituted and legitimised. Accordingly, there are three (four) different sorts of election: municipal, *Land*, federal (and European) elections, which are held every four or five years, according to the various electoral rules.

The political parties are active at every level of the State, and are the most important organisations for the development of political opinion, in that they present the voters with a variety of programmes and candidates, and compete for political office. Nowadays it is only at the level of local government that it is still possible to win a political mandate without the support of a political party. At the level of the *Länder* and the federal state the parties effectively have a complete monopoly of political representation.

The various strata of state organisation as a whole can be seen as a system of vertical power distribution and control. This is complemented at each level by a horizontal distribution. Above all, the federal and *Land* levels operate, in association with each other, as a system of double (horizontal and vertical) distribution and control of power; therein lies one of the most important constitutional functions of German federalism.

The independence and individual responsibility of local self-government as the lowest level of the entire federative structure of the State is laid down in Article 28, paragraph 2, of the *Grundgesetz*: 'Municipalities must be guaranteed the right to settle all local community matters on their own responsibility within the framework of the laws'. This right also applies to associations of municipalities: they too have the right to self-government within their own legal area of responsibility according to the laws.

As fundamental as this constitutional guarantee of self-government for municipalities, towns and districts is for the State's federative structure, it has to be admitted that developments since the beginning of the *Bundesrepublik* have tended more and more to increase the dependency of municipalities and towns on the *Länder* and the federal state, particularly in financial terms. This financial dependency has meant that *Land* and *Bund* respectively, through the exercise of their constitutional rights, have been able severely to restrict the political capabilities and freedom of action of the towns and municipalities. Nonetheless, municipal self-government remains, following its reorganisation after the far-reaching reforms of the municipalities in the early 1970s, the basis of Germany's federative order. Yet it is rarely at the forefront of political or even journalistic or academic concerns, which invariably focus on *Bund* and *Länder* and especially the distribution of power and jurisdiction between them. It is clear that, in spite of the fact that it is at the local level that the citizen can have the greatest say in his or her immediate political environment, municipal elections arouse comparatively less interest than *Landestag* and *Bundestag* elections. The turnout at municipal elections is generally low, undercut only by the European elections. It is apparent that, even at municipal level, voters believe *Land* and *Bund* politics have a greater impact on them personally than do municipal politics .

3. The central problem of federalism has two aspects: first the distribution of responsibilities and functions between the centre (*Bund*) and individual *Länder*; second, the problem of letting the *Länder* participate in federal policy decisions through a special federal organ in a fair and appropriate way.

When the *Bundesrepublik* was founded there was much debate about the right way to approach these two constitutional problems. In both cases several possible solutions were considered. The question of the distribution of responsibilities and functions revolved above all around the question of finance. Two variations had already been tried - with mixed success - at earlier stages in German history. First, at the time of Bismarck, when the *Reich* as the central power had remained financially dependent on the *Länder*. Second, during the Weimar Republic, when the *Länder* were, in the end, disastrously dependent on the *Reich* in financial terms - disastrous in the sense that this one-sided financial relationship left the political independence and freedom of action of the *Länder* seriously weakened. Therefore, in the latter stages of the Weimar Republic (1930-33) they were no longer able to offer any significant resistance to the rise of National Socialism. This led to the simultaneous collapse of the Weimar Republic and Hitler's seizure of power. The National Socialist State that resulted was organised in a centralist mode; it therefore stood in contradiction to every tradition of German state formation and organisation.

As a result of this historical experience, the founders of the *Bundesrepublik* constitution attempted a far-reaching revision of the federative structure, in order to avoid the problems and dangers of the earlier arrangements. Above all the distribution of responsibilities in the field of legislation and public functions required reorganisation. An essential precondition for this was an improved financial constitution, which would avoid the (one-sided) dependency both of the *Bund* on the *Länder* as well as the reverse dependency of the *Länder* on the *Bund*, and would guarantee for both actors as large as possible a measure of financial autonomy.

As far as the distribution of legislative responsibility is concerned, German federalism does not follow the concept of strict division (as in the USA) but rather a combination of functions. There is a tri-partite distinction between legislation which is exclusive to *Bund* and *Länder* respectively, framework legislation for the *Bund*, and concurrent legislation affecting both *Bund* and *Länder*. What this distinction means in detail is itemised and defined in Paragraph VII of the constitution. So for example the subjects of the *Bund's* exclusive legislation in Article 73 are itemised in just as much detail as the subjects of concurrent legislation. The list of subject matter is long and the sphere of concurrent legislation has been enlarged constantly over the years - to the benefit of the *Bund*. For example: 'The *Bund* has a right to legislate in this sphere, so long as there exists a need for federal law ruling' (Article 72 of the *Grundgesetz*). In this context, the *Länder* may only legislate as long as 'the *Bund* does not exercise its right to legislate'. However, this has been the case less and less frequently in the history of the *Bundesrepublik*. The *Bund* has exercised that right just as thoroughly for concurrent legislation as in the field of framework legislation. The main reason for this development is to be found in Article 72, (paragraphs 2, 3): 'the maintenance of uniform living standards'. The *Länder* have also called upon this principle in support of their activity in those areas where they can claim exclusive legislative competence, for example in the sphere of cultural and education policy (schools, colleges, science, culture, etc). By setting up a standing conference of education ministers, for example, the *Länder* have created for themselves a special organ of self-coordination (without participation from the *Bund*) capable of monitoring the uniformity of standards in the field of education and culture. It was entirely logical that the *Länder* should create specialist committees (*Bildungsrat* and *Wissenschaftsrat*), for the coordination and integration of education and science policies, and that in the end the *Bund* should bring this increasingly important area within the sphere of its own framework legislation (e.g. framework legislation for colleges) and within its own financial ambit. This example shows that development was constantly in the direction of a unitary state (*Unitarisierung*); hence the talk of a 'unitary federal Republic' or of 'cooperative federalism', in order to describe this growing tendency towards standardisation in the German federative system. The exclusive responsibilities of the *Länder* have been reduced in number, and have become more restricted in scope. Now they are more or less limited to the regulation of the police and education; and even in these areas the *Bund* has become increasingly active through its framework legislation.

However, it is notable that, as the legislative independence of the *Länder* has been reduced, there has been a rise in the responsibilities of the *Bundesrat* at federal level, for the growing share of concurrent and framework legislation taken over from the *Bund* is composed, naturally enough, of subjects for legislation which require agreement because they concern the interests of the *Länder* and cannot be enacted without the agreement of the *Bundesrat*. The number of such subjects has grown from one legislative period to the next, and amounts to about 75% or 80% of laws – a clear indication of the considerably strengthened position of the *Bundesrat* in the legislative process of the *Bundesrepublik*.

The integration of responsibilities between *Bund* and *Länder* can be seen in another important area, that of administration. Chapter VIII of the *Grundgesetz* rules specifically on 'the implementation of federal law and federal administration'. It is in this area that the *Länder* chiefly exercise their specific responsibilities, for the *Bund* has separate administrative responsibility for only very few spheres of activity, such as foreign affairs (diplomacy), federal financial administration, federal railways, major traffic and transport administration (air, roads, water), the federal postal service, Federal Border Guards and a few other minor areas, and similarly also in the federal armed forces and their administration. In general, Article 83 is valid for the implementation of administration: 'the implementation of federal laws is the concern of the *Länder*, so long as the *Grundgesetz* does not determine or allow otherwise'. Essentially, the *Länder* have an overall responsibility and obligation to set up administrative authorities to undertake the functions of the executive. Finally it should be remembered that, through close cooperation of *Bund* and *Länder* ('cooperative federalism') a growing number of 'joint tasks' have appeared, which the *Bund* contributes to at a planning and finance level. This means that the *Bund* plays a part in the implementation of *Länder* tasks if these are relevant to the country as a whole and if the *Bund's* contribution is necessary for the improvement of living standards. The most important spheres of activity for these joint tasks are: construction and extension of colleges, and structural improvements to the economy and agriculture of the region.

The *Bundesrat*, as the organ of federal legislation, has been able significantly to increase its political influence through the institution of these joint tasks, while as a result the *Länder* have, for their part, suffered a loss of political independence. This has become a significant political factor, especially in a situation where, as at present, the majority in the *Bundesrat* is at odds with the *Bundestag*. In this case, the opposition which is in a minority in Parliament can use its majority in the *Bundestag* to continue its opposition, and to force the government to compromise, for it is simply not possible to arrive at a legislative decision without the agreement of the *Bundesrat*. When the two chambers are unable to come to agreement on a bill, then the mediation committee, composed equally of members of the *Bundestag* and the *Bundesrat*, is called in, and has, so far, managed to find a compromise in most disputes between government and opposition.

The system of division of responsibilities between *Bund* and *Länder* requires an appropriate division of tax revenues. In this respect, the financial constitution (or

Finanzwesen) represents a central element of the federal state constitution as a whole (cf the *Grundgesetz*, Section X, '*Das Finanzwesen*' (Art. 104a – 115)).

The *Finanzwesen* contains various rulings of fundamental significance for the federative structure: first in relation to legislative responsibility in financial and taxation matters. Since the reform of 1969, the *Bund* has very much the major role here; nonetheless, federal tax laws as a rule need the agreement of the *Länder* in the *Bundesrat*.

The allocation of tax revenue (vertical redistribution) is of central importance. Article 106 sets out in detail which taxes and state income the *Bund* is entitled to, and which the *Länder*. It is interesting that the most important taxes (income, corporation, and sales (VAT) tax) are apportioned jointly to the *Bund* and the *Länder*: income and corporation tax are divided equally between *Bund* and *Länder*, while the distribution of sales or value added tax is determined by federal law (with the agreement of the *Bundesrat*), and the ratio may be varied according to circumstances. This has happened recently in connection with the so-called 'solidarity agreement' ('*Solidarpakt*') for the new *Länder* and has altered in favour of the *Länder*.

We need, though, to remember that the districts (*Gemeinden*), which are the lowest level of the federative system and which would otherwise receive only a very small provision from their own taxes (mainly trade taxes), receive a share of the income tax revenue of the *Länder*; the precise size is determined by federal law for the entire *Bundesrepublik*. Since there are often considerable differences between the *Länder* with regard to size, economic strength and consequently tax yield, there is a process of 'horizontal financial redistribution'. In this way, it is intended that 'variations in the financial strength of the *Länder* can be suitably evened out' (Article 107, paragraph 1 of the *Grundgesetz*). Accordingly, a distinction is made between those *Länder* which are financially weak and therefore entitled to redistribution in their favour, and those which are financially strong and are therefore obliged to contribute; equalisation between the two is carried out on a legal basis. It is significant that, in the course of the history of the *Bundesrepublik*, variations in economic development since 1949 have caused substantial shifts in the relationship between the two categories. Some *Länder* which once belonged to the contributing group have now joined those in receipt of redistributed income; other *Länder* which initially benefited from redistribution now find themselves obliged to contribute. Regional economic policy has had differing effects here; old, classic industrial regions (such as the *Ruhrgebiet*) have declined in importance, while new industrial regions, with the most modern electronic technology, have emerged. The original economic discrepancy between North and South has long since evolved into a distinction between South West and North East; today therefore Baden Würtemberg and Hessen are at the summit of economic power in the *Bundesrepublik*. Since unification, the five new *Länder* are grouped together at the foot of the table. Their economic and financial plight is currently still so great that they have not yet been admitted to the federal system of financial redistribution. The essential support which they require is being provided until 1995 by the 'German Unity Fund' ('*Fonds Deutsche Einheit*'), set up by the *Bund* and the *Länder*. Unsurprisingly, the federal financial constitution remains very much a subject of controversy. With the political situation in a constant state of flux, the material and financial challenges, big and small, to the joint policies of *Bund* and *Länder* are subject to endless change. At the moment, with the process of German unification underway, they seem particularly big and, for a long time to come, will continue to represent probably the greatest challenge to the federative system of the *Bundesrepublik*.

The second controversial point concerns the institutional framework within which the *Länder* can participate in federal policy-making, and here too there is a number of possible variations. On one side, the American Senate principle could be followed, according to which the population of the *Länder* would democratically elect a certain number of representatives (senators), who would constitute a senate as a second parliamentary chamber. This would then participate in the federal state decision-making and legislative process alongside the representative body. Alternatively, it would be possible to follow the *Rat* principle, under which, the governments of the *Länder* form a sort of second chamber through which their interests are looked after at federal level.

The founding fathers of the *Bundesrepublik* constitution came down in favour of the *Rat* solution not least on the grounds of old German traditions and experiences. The *Bundesrat* as the federal organ of the *Länder* is not elected, but consists of representatives of the *Länder* governments, whose task it is to look after the interests of the *Länder*. Each *Land* therefore has a number of votes according to its size ('Each *Land* has at least three votes: *Länder* with more than five million inhabitants have four, *Länder* with more than six million inhabitants five. *Länder* with more than seven million inhabitants have six' (Article 51, paragraph 2 of the *Grundgesetz*)), and when there is a ballot these votes may only be cast en bloc. The *Reich* under Bismarck and the Weimar Republic had operated under the same *Rat* principle. At the assembly which decided on the form of the constitution, (the *'Parlamentarische Rat'*), only a small minority of members was in favour of the American senate principle, which therefore had no chance of being adopted.

It is extremely hard to assess whether, overall, this was a sensible decision; the criteria to be applied vary according to circumstances: with the criterion of efficiency in mind, the *Rat* principle has to be favoured, to the extent that it is to be expected that the *Länder* governments, with the support of their ministerial bureaucracy, can work more effectively and efficiently in the interests of their *Länder* than a few representatives whose loyalty as a rule is primarily to their party and who therefore pursue national rather than regional goals. Under the criterion of democratisation, the senate principle finds equally strong favour, since senate members are directly elected by the inhabitants of their *Land* and therefore can claim direct democratic legitimacy for their task.

If we compare the achievements of the representative body of the German *Länder* (the *Bundesrat*), constituted along federative lines, with other federative second chambers in Europe or elsewhere, then its efficiency and quality cannot be overstated. Furthermore, it must be stressed that the *Bundesrat*, in the course of developments from 1949 to the present day, has been able substantially to enhance its political position and significance. Above all, its share of the *Bund's* legislative activity has constantly grown. There are fewer and fewer parliamentary bills which are not declared by the *Bundesrat* to be in need of its agreement. This tendency has at times been so much in evidence that the federal constitutional court has had to limit the power of the *Bundesrat* to impose the requirement for agreement on bills, in favour of the federal government.

We are faced therefore today with a paradoxical situation with regard to both basic decisions; as far as the regulations concerning the responsibilities of *Bund* and *Länder* are concerned, this development has clearly worked to the benefit overall of federal responsibilites. The *Länder* - and particularly the *Landtage*, the *Länder* parliaments - have declined in importance as political decision-making authorities. As for the involvement of the *Länder* at the federal level - through the *Bundesrat* with its *Länder* representatives - the result has been a considerable expansion of the need for agreement and therefore a noticeable strengthening of the role of the *Bundesrat*.

Recently, in connection with German unification and European integration, the *Länder* have adopted common initiatives with the aim of extending still further the significance of the *Länder* in federal politics; this aim is served particularly by the revision of article 23 of the constitution, which is intended to increase the participation of the *Länder* in federal decisions concerning Europe. This article has yet to be adopted.

3. The Constitutional Function of Federalism today
We have seen that the re-introduction of federalism as a basic principle of the *Grundgesetz* has been brought about by considerations which are partly traditional and historical and partly constitutional.

The German political system always had a federalist tradition; this corresponded to the varied patterns of state formation on German territory since the Middle Ages. Furthermore, the attempts at nation-state integration in the nineteenth century could only be made within the existing federal structure.

Attention was focused particularly strongly on constitutional considerations after the Second World War because of the unfortunate fate of the Weimar Republic and the experiences with the totalitarian National Socialist state. The weak position of the *Länder* in relation to the *Reich* in the Weimar system, the way in which they were rapidly brought into line during the NS seizure of power, as well as the subsequent definitive elimination of the federative structure of the German *Reich* and the setting up of a totalitarian dictatorship - all these were experiences which stimulated constitutional discussions in the post-war period and also promoted the reinstatement of the federative component in the formation of the German state. Against this background of contemporary history, the re-establishment of the *Länder* and of federalism should be seen as part of a many-sided reflection on constitutional matters, the most important aspects of which are those which relate to democracy and the rule of law.

1. The democratisation of Germany, as conceived by the victors in the Potsdam agreement of August 1945, gave prominence to the view that German involvement with democracy and democratic rules should be allowed to develop from the ground up, that is first at the lower, communal level, then at the level of the *Länder* and only then at the level of the state as a whole. This meant that this concept of democracy formed the basis for a federative state organisation at three levels: commune, *Länder*, *Bund*. Democratisation was thought of essentially as an educative process, which would be developed from elementary and comprehensible situations in the communal sphere, evolving gradually towards more complex and difficult situations at *Länder* and state level. The new federative structure was enormously influential in the way that it determined the various levels of this educative process.

The division of Germany which rapidly followed steered this process of democratisation in different directions and along different paths in West and East Germany. The early GDR (1949-52) was indeed a state constructed on federative lines, with a constitution closely modelled on that of the Weimar Republic; however, once the goal of the construction of socialism along Soviet lines had been proclaimed, then this original federative concept lost all meaning and was replaced by a centralist-bureaucratic concept.

In West Germany, this process developed differently; here the federative structure was of fundamental constitutional importance for the formation of the new *Bundesrepublik*, both under pressure from the Western Occupying Powers and also because of the desire for democracy on the part of West German politicians. The fact that Germany had traditionally had a federal system certainly played an important supporting role, but it was not in itself a decisive one. At the same time preoccupations with constitutional order loomed large - because of the experiences, mentioned above, with the totalitarian dictatorship of National Socialism. There can be no doubt that a federative system has a strengthening and intensifying effect on democracy through its various political levels; seen in this light, there is a positive correlation between the principles of federalism and democracy in the *Grundgesetz*. In practice the federal system, with its various political levels (communes, *Länder*, *Bund*), brings about a multiplication of democratic institutions and corresponding opportunities for democratic participation. At each of these levels, there are parliaments and governments and other political authorities, for which appropriate staff have to be recruited. Democratic elections make their contribution too, and political parties gain considerably in areas of activity and influence through the state's distinctive federative structure, since they do not just take part in the process of political opinion-forming nationwide but are also active at communal and *Länder* level. It quite frequently occurs that parties which are part of the opposition at national level have charge of majorities and governments at *Länder* level, and vice versa. This produces a substantially deeper and more favourable integration of the political parties in the political system and, at the same time, opportunities for politicians and political new blood to participate in the political process at all three levels. Most prominent German politicians in the post-war period including, for example, former Federal Chancellors, had as a rule been able to gain political experience at the communal or *Länder* level. It is also very much the case that federal politicians, after careers as members of parliament or even ministers have then taken on leading positions, for example as Prime Minister of a *Land* or as mayor of a large city. This means that the various political levels of the federal system are inter-changeable one with the other, and there is an exchange of personnel in both an upward and a downward direction.

This intensification of democracy also affects the political role and opportunities for participation of ordinary citizens. To the extent that he or she is simultaneously citizen of a town, a *Land*, and the *Bundesrepublik*, he or she has a civic responsibilty at all three levels (and now also on the European level). In concrete terms, that means that, over a period of four or five years, there will be opportunities to vote four times; that he or she will be able to have a say in the make up of parliaments and (indirectly) of governments four times every four or five years. In the past, the citizens of the *Bundesrepublik* have readily accepted these opportunities. They have however attributed varying degrees of importance to the different elections; as a result, communal elections attract fewer voters, elections to the *Länder* parliaments attract more, with clearly the largest turnout being for elections to the federal parliament. In this latter case, the turnout is of the order of 90%; it is only very recently that the number of abstentions in all forms of election has risen dramatically, as a result of disenchantment with politics and parties, and the turnout has fallen alarmingly. So far it is unclear whether these abstentions can be put down to politically motivated protest rather than to a growing political apathy. Whichever it is (the forthcoming 1994 elections will probably provide a better indication of the real reasons), there can be no doubt that the federative structure of the *Bundesrepublik* gives a significant impetus to democratic participation, in terms both of breadth and depth. Therein lies one of the most important constitutional functions of that structure. And in this respect federalism has proved its worth in Germany.

2. There are, however, other constitutional factors to consider, not least the principle of the state as embodiment of the rule of law. This relates principally to the theme of the division and control of power, functions which, it can be argued, are much enhanced by the state's federal structure. The accuracy of this thesis is easily verifiable: in brief, the classic horizontal division and control of power is completed by an equally effective vertical division. In concrete terms this means that the traditional horizontal division between Parliament and government and the courts, between legislative, executive and judiciary, is extended and deepened by the federal structure's multiple vertical division between communes, *Länder* and *Bund*.

In the context of the principle of the rule of law, this system provides not only a double division of power but also an enlargement and safeguard of individual freedoms in the face of state power. This double division increases the opportunities for protection under the law. Political despotism can be more readily, and more rapidly, kept in check. This is also the main reason why dictatorial or totalitarian regimes always ensure the abolition or destruction of the federative system as a first priority (c.f. NS regime; DDR regime).

Federalism has proved its worth, too, in the field of culture and education policy where, as we have seen, the *Länder* have a particular responsibility. The diversity of educational and cultural provision in Germany is well known. In contrast to Great Britain and France, the *Bundesrepublik* does not have a dominant cultural centre; whether Berlin, as capital, can take on this role is questionable and may not be entirely desirable. Germany's diversity in this field has its roots in the old princely and bourgeois traditions, but has been underlined by modern federalism (it is an area in which the *Länder* compete with each other), and can be seen as a positive constitutional value at a time when the principle of multiplicity tends to be subordinated to the principle of unity (and centrality). Also, it must be remembered that this cultural diversity is reflected in the spheres of education and science, schools and universities. The pattern of university education in the *Bundesrepublik* is thus very pluralistic. The support and extension of universities and colleges are primarily a task for the *Länder*, although for years the *Bund* has contributed to the allocation of financial resources.

One final justification for federalism can be found in the constitutional discussions which took place in Germany in the aftermath of 1945, and it is one which has taken on a new significance in the current context of European integration. This is the principle of subsidiarity. It was in part the social teaching of the Catholic Church which served as a basis for the decision by the founding fathers of the German constitution in 1949 to enshrine subsidiarity as a constitutional principle. Specifically, the expression of this principle was found in the papal encyclical '*Quadragesimo anno*' of 1931. This declares that 'that which an individual can achieve on his own initiative and by his own ability, should not be taken away from him and arrogated instead to a function of society'. It is generally in contravention of justice that 'that which lower or smaller communities are able to achieve and put to good use should be claimed for the benefit of the wider community'. For 'each and every social activity is of course by its very nature and by definition subsidiary; it should support the constituent parts of society, but should never crush or absorb them.' Quite clearly, this general socio-political maxim is a very reasonable one, and provides an outstanding justification of the federal principle with its vertical differentiation of power. It can also offer a useful critical standard for judging the extent to which the centre may at any time legitimately intervene in areas for which individual federal entities have responsibility. It is equally clear that, in the political reality of today's *Bundesrepublik*, the implementation of the subsidiarity principle through the central state is a source of difficulty and that, in the balance between *Bund* and *Länder*, the weight has clearly tended to shift in favour of the *Bund*. This does not mean, however, that the question of subsidiarity has been settled and put to one side. On the contrary, it remains valid as a normative constitutional principle for federalism.

Thus the constitutional principles of democracy and the rule of law are very much in harmony with federalism, providing reciprocal strength and support.

In contrast, however, the principles of federalism and the social state do not fit harmoniously together; there is no denying the tensions between them, which are visible throughout the *Bundesrepublik* system. In essence, these tensions arise from the fact that it is hard to reconcile the basic values of multiplicity and uniformity on which federalism and the social state are based. And this in spite of the fact that, as we have already seen, Article 20 of the *Grundgesetz* includes the phrase 'social federal state'.

While federalism is founded on the concepts of plurality and multiplicity, the social state is based on equality and uniformity; it establishes as the primary policy objective the 'maintenance of legal and economic unity, especially the maintenance of uniform living standards' within the territory of a *Land*. (Article 72, 2, paragraph 3).

We have already pointed out how, over a period of time, the independence and responsibility of the *Länder* have been considerably reduced, with a corresponding increase in central state responsibility for action, as a result of the constitutional position of the social state. This tension appears unavoidable, for the social or welfare state seems to have a 'natural', inherent tendency towards centralism or centralisation. The increasing modern need for public welfare provision accentuates the trend to sacrifice the variety of regional and federal arrangements in public life in favour of the strict law of standardisation which the pursuit of equality demands.

3. Federalism and restructuring. 'Nothing lasts longer than the temporary.' This sentence which, until recently (up to German unification in 1990), was often used to describe the political system of the *Bundesrepublik* and the stability of its constitutional structure, is no less applicable to the *Länder* of the *Bundesrepublik*. Created after the Second World War by the Occupying Powers within the context of the four occupation zones, they were for the most part accidental and artificial constructs. In hardly any instance did they reflect historical traditions or former regional or even state affiliations. The only exceptions are the two Hanseatic towns of Bremen and Hamburg as well as, above all, the free state of Bavaria; these evolved as legitimate, historical, political entities, and it is notable

that they have therefore been able to create their own political identity.

The somewhat haphazard and provisional way in which the *Länder* were initially set up after 1945, led to the provision in the second of the three 'Frankfurt Documents' (1948) for a reform of the *Länder* boundaries, and also to the formulation in Article 29 paragraph 2 of the *Grundgesetz*: 'the federal region is to be restructured by federal law, in consideration of regional solidarity, historical and cultural affiliations, economic efficiency, and social structure. The restructuring should create *Länder* which can fulfil their incumbent tasks effectively according to their size and productivity.' [NB the restructuring of the *Länder* as stipulated by the constitution (permitting alterations to both the borders and the number of *Länder*) does not contradict the 'eternity' guarantee of Article 79, paragraph 3 of the constitution; this guarantee relates to the principle of the federal state, not the number of *Länder* or their individual responsibilities.]

So far, nothing has come of this restructuring stipulation, in spite of numerous declarations of intent, proposals, plans, blueprints, etc. Only once in the forty-year history of the *Bundesrepublik* has there been a partial reform of the federalist system, in the southwest of the country: in the early 1950s three small *Länder*, Baden, Württemberg-Baden and Württemberg-Hohenzollern, located partly in the American and partly in the French sector, merged to form the new 'southwest state' of Baden-Württemberg (with its seat of government in Stuttgart). That is how it has remained to this day, in spite of numerous commissions, reports, plans and proposals. Those *Länder* which have been in existence since the foundation of the *Bundesrepublik* have proved themselves, for all their inadequacies, to be so stable and lasting that all restructuring plans, which in any case have often been based on questionable logic, have up to now remained unsuccessful. This resistance to all such plans, which invariably allowed for a (more or less drastic) reduction in the number of *Länder*, can be explained in part at least by the instinct for self-preservation displayed by many *Länder* politicians, who are naturally aware that the break-up or merging of individual *Länder* would mean the loss of political office and would therefore put their own political careers in jeopardy. As a result of this political inertia, many restructuring plans have disappeared from public discussion, and the constitutional stipulation set out in Article 29, paragraph 2 has remained unfulfilled from 1949 to German unification in 1990!

Meanwhile, German unification has brought about a new situation: the question of restructuring the federal regions is once more on the agenda. The re-federalisation of East Germany has provided, in addition, a good opportunity to revive the idea of restructuring the federal regions as a whole, in accordance with the requirements of Article 29, para 2 of the constitution.

Nevertheless, it is fairly easy to predict that this new attempt at restructuring the federal regions, which will be contested in part with the old arguments and essentially old plans, will not lead to any concrete new reorganisation of the *Bundesrepublik*. Nothing more than a partial reform is in prospect: Article 5 of the German Unification Treaty provides for the merging of Brandenburg and Berlin in one federal *Land*. But even this partial new ruling has remained stalled at the level of preliminary discussions. It is clearly open to question whether it will come to pass before the end of the century. At present, especially in the new *Länder*, there is an abundance of difficult and more immediate problems in practically every sphere of internal German politics. In all probability the task of restructuring the entire federal system will be postponed indefinitely in the face of these current problems.

4. German unification and federalism. It is hard to imagine any event in Germany's recent past which has had as much significance for national as well as European history as German unification.

At a time when hardly any politicians or citizens of the *Bundesrepublik* considered 'German reunification', which was laid down in the preamble to the *Grundgesetz* as a prime policy objective, to be a real possibility, the socialist camp broke up at breathtaking speed, socialism as both an ideology and a political system collapsed throughout Europe and therefore also in the DDR. The opportunity for the reunification of Germany appeared, then, quite unexpectedly; the citizens of the DDR, who had just brought about the surrender of their socialist masters with the words '*Wir sind das Volk*', now clearly expressed their political will for a rapid national amalgamation of the *Bundesrepublik* and the DDR with the new slogan '*Wir sind ein Volk*'. In the autumn of 1989 and spring of 1990, this political will built up such a momentum that it swept aside all resistance to German unification, but also all in-between measures.

It is important for our theme that in this process there was also a revival of the federal idea in East Germany. The collapse of the centralist SED regime, which had abolished the original federal structure of the DDR in the early 1950s for reasons of political power, brought with it tendencies towards regionalisation on the basis of the old traditional *Länder* in the DDR. Democratisation and federalisation therefore came into being simultaneously as political options for the citizens' movement at the end of the DDR. The re-establishment of the former *Länder* and of communal self-government therefore formed part of the primary political demands of the citizens' movement in East Germany, among others expressed in the 'round table' negotiations. The political parties and democratic groups which were anxious to gain influence on the democratisation process in this first phase, could not ignore demands for the federalisation of the DDR. Thus the first and only freely-elected and democratically legitimised DDR government, which followed the *Volkskammer* elections on 18 May 1990, announced as one of its first aims 'the creation of a federative republic'. Accordingly a 'Ministry for regional and communal affairs' was set up. The concept of the re-federalisation of the DDR provided for the re-founding of the *Länder* 'on the lines of the pre-1952 structure', as well as the establishment of a '*Länderkammer*'. Several different models of federal structure, with varying numbers of *Länder*, were discussed in the *Volkskammer*. This discussion was soon caught up in the slipstream of the reunification discussions. In the end that led to a majority view in favour of the re-establishment of the five former *Länder*, Mecklenburg-Vorpommern, Brandenburg, Sachsen, Sachsen-Anhalt and Thüringen, in spite of considerable misgivings over the existence and effectiveness of these *Länder*. On the basis of these discussions, the DDR Volkskammer formulated a law (*Ländereinführungsgesetz*) which set the date of 14 October 1990 for the formation of five *Länder* and laid down the rules for every essential aspect of the new federative structure of the DDR. These included the responsibilities of the *Länder*, the distribution of legislative and financial responsibilities, etc., and indeed the relationship to the *Grundgesetz* of the *Bundesrepublik*, in order to facilitate subsequent unification.

This process of refederalisation of the DDR was, however, overtaken by the speed of German unification. The *Ländereinführungsgesetz* should have come into force in the DDR on 14 October; yet on 3 October the unification of Germany through the accession of the DDR *Länder* to the *Bundesrepublik* was completed according to Article 23 of the *Grundgesetz*. The governments of the two German states had agreed this in the 'treaty between the *Bundesrepublik Deutschland* and the *Deutsche Demokratische Republik* on the restoration of German unity' (Unification Treaty of 31 August 1990). As early as 1 July 1990, the treaty establishing economic, monetary, and social union, by which the German Mark (DM) became the official currency of the DDR, had come into force.

In order that the federative structure of the *Bundesrepublik* should not be put at risk by the speed of this re-unification process, the West German *Länder* had proposed, on 5 July 1990, a number of parameters (*Eckpunkten*) for federalism in a united Germany. Their intention was to underline emphatically the federative character of re-united Germany, while at the same time speaking up for the extension of federalism, and particularly for a strengthening of the position of the *Länder* in the constitutional system.

The new *Länder* could only be properly constituted once unification had taken place, following the *Landtag* elections on 14 October 1990 and the formation of the *Länder* parliaments, which at the same time had to function as constituent assemblies. These imposed provisional constitutions on the *Länder* and decided on the capital of each *Land*.

It was only after the formation of the new *Länder* governments that the *Bundesrat*, representing the *Länder*, was able to assemble. This it did on 9 November 1990, with the representatives of sixteen rather than the previous eleven *Land* governments. Thus the refederalisation of the former DDR and the integration of the five new *Länder* into the federative system of the *Bundesrepublik* was completed. The problem now is to breath life into this newly-integrated structure, and to make it possible for the new *Länder* to take their rightful constitutional place within the federative constitutional system of the *Bundesrepublik*. This may well not be easy; the generally impoverished condition of the new *Länder* means that, for the foreseeable future, they will be in an extremely weak position and in need of help, above all in the form of financial support on the part of the *Bund* and the old *Bundesländer*. It is doubtful, then, at the very least, whether the increase in the number of *Länder* through the unification process can produce a qualitative strengthening of federalism. The dependency of the new *Länder* is enormous, and is bound to last for a long time.

4. Current problems of German Federalism
Recent significant problems affecting German federalism stem from two different political developments:

    -first from the process of German unification,

    -second from the process of European integration.

Both problem areas represent considerable challenges to traditional German federalism. There is no prospect of a straightforward, rapid and satisfactory solution to either, especially since the political system in the *Bundesrepublik* is currently undergoing a difficult endurance test, perhaps even the most difficult in its history.

1. We have seen that German unification followed the accession of the five *Länder* of the former DDR in accordance with Article 23, which made possible the accession of 'other parts of Germany' to the *Bundesrepublik*. Thus the number of *Länder* rose from the former eleven to sixteen. Through this form of accession,

German unification became, among other things, a problem of German federalism, to the extent that the new *Länder* were/are to be included in the German federal system. In terms of constitutional law, this means giving the new *Länder* the same status and the same rights as those possessed by the old *Länder* since the founding of the *Bundesrepublik*, including the revival of previous *Land* traditions, the forming of suitable *Land* constitutions, political systems and parties, etc.

For the new *Länder* to achieve formal legal parity with the old *Länder* they require – along with their formation as political entities with constitutions, parliaments, governments, etc. – equal status within the framework of the *Bund*. This is necessary in view of their involvement with the federal state financial constitution, with the distribution of legislative responsibilities both in the *Bundesrat* and as *Länder* representatives at the federal level.

Bringing the new *Länder* in line with the old, as political entities with democratic constitutions and institutions, with their democratic legitimisation through elections and with their inclusion as members with equal rights in the *Bundesrat*, created no significant problems. However, the alignment of the new *Länder* with the old, in the field of the financial system is causing considerable difficulties. The problem is that all five new *Länder* are relatively poor and weak and will be seriously in need of substantial and guaranteed long-term support from the *Bund* and the old *Länder* after forty years of a socialist regime. In view of the present serious difference of level, it was not possible for them to be admitted immediately into the financial equalisation system of the *Bundesrepublik*. Instead, the unification treaty of 1990 provides for the new *Länder* to be financially supported until 1994 by the 'German Unity Fund' (*Fonds Deutsche Einheit*) set up specifically for that purpose. In the period 1990-94, a total of 115 billion DM will have been made available by the *Bundesrepublik* (*Bund* and old *Länder*) – with little visible sign of success to date. That is why further efforts are called for, leading amongst other things to the so-called 'solidarity pact' of *Bund* and *Länder*. In years to come a gigantic redistribution from west to east will be required, in order to re-establish equal living standards in Germany as a whole. To start with, this means a fall in the living standards and prosperity of the old *Länder*. The crux of these efforts is the economic reconstruction of East Germany, whose industry faces the most severe difficulties in all areas because of mismanagement during the DDR era. As it happens, the economic problems of unification have clearly been grossly underestimated by the federal government. This has led to many misjudgements and poor planning of reconstruction policies, resulting in the collapse of many industries and growing unemployment in the new *Länder*. The consequences of these problems for German political culture are incalculable. In the new *Länder* particularly – once the initial euphoria of German unification had worn off – disillusion has been widespread. It is unfortunate that the construction of a new democratic way of life has coincided with an economic recession and a crisis in living standards. It will not be easy to win back the trust in democratic politics and a democratic political system which has already been lost. These negative trends also have a negative effect on the acceptance of federalism and its achievements.

2. The process of European integration also constitutes a serious problem for German federalism. The *Länder* are under threat, in terms of their decision-making power, from the progressive transfer of responsibilities away from the federal government towards Brussels. Their participation in political decisions has

been severely reduced also at the federal level, their responsibilities eroded and their substance threatened. There is a danger that matters of particular concern to the *Länder* will remain unconsidered. In this situation, which has led to considerable tension between *Bund* and *Länder*, the *Länder* have pursued three means of defence against the obvious danger to their political existence:

— First, they have established their presence at the centre of EC decision-making by setting up special offices in Brussels and, as a form of *Länder* lobby group, attempted to gain direct influence there on European policy-making.

— Second, they have sought to improve their position in the European decision-making process in relation to the ratification of the Maastricht Treaty, an attempt which finds its expression within the *Bundesrepublik* in the projected (but not yet adopted) revision of Article 23 of the Constitution. Here it is expressly stated that 'in the matter of European union, ... the *Bundestag* and, through the *Bundesrat*, the *Länder*, cooperate. The federal government must keep the *Bundestag* and the *Bundesrat* comprehensively and rapidly informed'. It is later stated: 'the *Bundesrat* is to participate in the development of informed opinion in the *Bund* (on European questions), in so far as it is able to participate at an appropriate internal level or that the *Länder* are internally responsible.

— A third possibility, or opportunity, to safeguard and perhaps even to strengthen the position of German federalism within the framework of European integration has arisen recently through the increased coordination of regionalist efforts at a European level, efforts in which the *Länder*, through their initiatives, have played a leading part. For a long time the *Länder* scorned the prospect of co-operating with regionalist groupings and organisations in other countries because they did not view them as having genuine constitutional status. Latterly, however, they have overcome these shortsighted inhibitions. They are co-operating with other European regions of varying constitutional status and trying to institutionalise, in an official 'Committee of the Regions', the specific needs and interests of each European region. Behind this lies the awareness that the traditional nation states are often unsuited, as members of the European Community, to an appreciation of regional interests, that these regional problems require the representation of their own interests through the regions themselves. Within this context, the *Länder* of the *Bundesrepublik* can play a particularly meaningful exemplary role, as developed political entities with constitutional status. This role could become even more significant if in the future Austria and Switzerland, with their similarly structured federalist *Länder*, were to be admitted to membership of the EC. The European Community, which is moving towards political union, will probably only be able to turn this political union into a reality if it is a federative one, in which the regions are granted an independent and responsible role at a lower level. The introduction of the subsidiarity principle in the Maastricht Treaty also points in this direction. Therefore, in this newest treaty on European integration, a socio-philosophical principle has been introduced that stems recognisably from the social teachings of the Catholic Church. It makes the normative statement, which is as it were grounded in natural law, that the lower and smaller unit takes precedence in being allowed to function according to its natural functional capacity. As a result, these smaller or lower units, the regions or *Länder* in the federally structured entity of Europe, are guaranteed preferential freedom of manoeuvre when it comes to determining what they are.

5. Conclusion

In the mid fifties, it was not uncommon to hear calls for the abolition of a federalism seen as obsolete, faced with the tremendous processes of industrial and economic development of the old *Bundesrepublik*. On the one hand federalism was seen as a hindrance to prosperity and progress, on the other as an unnecessary and expensive antiquity, with its multiplication of state institutions (parliaments, governments etc.) at the level of the *Länder*.

This sort of reaction is no longer heard. In recent years there has been a fundamental change to the long-held belief in the supreme value of state unity as opposed to traditional and regional variety. Paradoxically, in the age of trans- and supra-national co-operation and integration, the level of regions and *Länder* has gained in significance throughout Europe. The view is widely accepted, that those nation states organised along the most centralist lines have become doubly problematical today: they appear too small to deal with the big problems, and too big to deal with the small ones. In the first case, it is trans- and supra-national integration which can provide a response, in the second, the formation of regions and (trans-national) regional co-operative entities. The most recent European attempt at integration, embodied in the Maastricht Treaty, has taken this tendency into account through the introduction of the concept of subsidiarity. In the preamble to the treaty, the EC member states declare their common determination 'to continue the process of creating an ever-closer union among the peoples of Europe, where, in keeping with the principle of subsidiarity, decisions are taken as closely as possible to the citizens'.

This European development is naturally reflected at the level of the individual nation state. As far as the *Bundesrepublik* is concerned, this means that the principle of federalism enshrined in the German constitution can no longer be seen as politically outdated and irksome. On the contrary, both with regard to the further development of Europe as well as, most especially, to the process of the completion of German unification, the federative structure of the *Bundesrepublik* occupies a key position, and one which, with regard to other European states organised until now along centralist lines (e.g. Great Britain, Italy, France), could exert an important exemplary influence. This does not mean that the obvious problem areas of current German federalism can be overlooked; on the contrary, present discussions in the *Bundesrepublik* on the revision of the constitution contain, amongst other things, proposals for the reform of the federal system. For example, the revision of Article 23 of the *Grundgesetz* indicates that new rules will have to apply to the *Länder's* right to participate in European decision-making. The capacity for reform of the federal system in the *Bundesrepublik* will have a significant impact on its future. Rapid political change, both internal and external, is forcing federalism continually to adapt, through the modification of structures and procedures. With this vitality, the federalist principle can represent in the future, in co-operation with the other constitutional principles, an important determining factor in the political system of the *Bundesrepublik*. In today's world - and in spite of all efforts at integration - politico-constitutional developments point in the direction of diversity, and it is this which - to a far greater extent than uniformity - gives free rein to the expression of human experience and needs in all their variety.

Regionalism in Italy
Anna Bull

1. Introduction

The Italian regional question is threefold. It is important to distinguish between regions as administrative entities, regional policy, including regional development, and regionalism/federalism as a political movement and current of thought. In Italy all three have played a part in shaping national as well as local politics since Unification, although at different times and with alternate fortunes. Indeed, it is only in recent years that these different aspects of regionalism have all become deeply enmeshed and achieved prominence at one and the same time, the catalyst for this being the formation of new regionally-based political 'Leagues'.

The main issues arising from the Italian regional question are the following:
1. In terms of the regions themselves, the main issue at the time of Unification was whether to introduce a system of administrative centralisation or decentralisation. Despite the pressure put on the Government by some advocates of a federal state, the question of whether to grant the regions autonomy rather than some measure of administrative devolution of power was never seriously considered. By contrast, the issue has now shifted dramatically and revolves around the alternatives of introducing a federal system of government or granting the regions considerable further administrative and fiscal powers, eg. the right to impose their own taxes.
2. In terms of regionalism/federalism as a current of opinion capable of influencing party politics, the issue at the time of the *Risorgimento* was how best to reconcile and integrate so many different peoples and cultures. Today, after more than 130 years of political unity, a much higher degree of homogeneity has been achieved, but from the point of view of socio-economic development (and in very recent times also in terms of political behaviour) the country appears to be divided into three inter-regional 'blocks': the North, the Centre and the South. The old federalism of the regions has given way to the federalism of the macro-regions advocated by the Northern League party.
3. In terms of regional policy and regional development, the issue at the turn of the century was how to achieve a redistribution of resources in favour of the poorer and less developed regions of Italy (i.e. the South). The North was criticised for draining resources from the South through an unfair taxation system and spending a higher proportion of public funds in the more affluent North. After the Second World War the issue became how best to promote economic development in the South through the channelling of specially ear-marked State funds. Today it is the very idea of State-funded regional development which is in question.

To enable the reader to follow the historical development of these three aspects of Italian regionalism from Unification to the 1980s, I will first consider them separately. When discussing present-day Italy, however, I will consider regionalism as a single, though multi-faceted, issue precisely because, as I mentioned earlier, all the above aspects seem to have become inextricably linked.

EUROPA 1(2/3) 1994 69-83 © Intellect Ltd 1994

2. A historical survey
2.1 The regional system
2.1.1. The Unification period
At the time of Unification, the Italian Government was faced with the dilemma of administrative centralisation or decentralisation. In those days 'Piedmontisation', i.e., the hurried extension of Piedmontese legislation to the newly annexed Italian regions, was resented in the North as well as in the South, although perhaps not to the same degree. The Piedmontese and the Lombards were different peoples with very different political-historical experiences, and so were the Tuscans, Emilians, Sicilians, Neapolitans etc. Only 2.5% of the population knew Italian at the time of Unification, a figure that includes the Tuscans, upon whose dialect the national language was based (De Mauro, 1963, p. 43).

The diversity of Italy's component regions as well as growing resentment in the country against Piedmontisation convinced Cavour as well as many other Italian political leaders that some measure of devolution ought to be granted. Cavour himself was a believer in decentralisation although, in the words of Mack Smith, 'he hardly had time to make up his mind' (Mack Smith, 1968, p. 341). In this, as in other instances, the Liberal Governments of Italy genuinely professed certain ideals but in practice had to introduce something very different when faced with the reality of Italian society and politics.

A scheme of regional devolution – the Farini-Minghetti bill – was prepared in 1861 and approved unanimously by the Cabinet but later withdrawn when it became clear that centrifugal forces, particularly in Southern Italy, could jeopardise the newly unified kingdom. Cavour himself changed his mind after Unification, shortly before his death in June 1861: 'despite the fact that he continued to deplore centralisation as illiberal, expensive and inefficient, he had been compelled to modify his views when he saw the danger that Italy might fall apart if a uniform administrative system was not quickly imposed on the whole kingdom' (Mack Smith, 1985, p. 263).

The most pressing agenda for the Italian ruling class at the time was how to 'harmonise' regional differences. In this context both the supporters of a centralised state and those of a federal state (see 2.2 below) had a common aim, although they differed in what they saw as the means to achieve this aim, alternatively 'from above', i.e., through the imposition of a uniform and centralised state apparatus, or 'from below', i.e., through a slow process of amalgamation and progressive elimination of local/regional differences. That the solution adopted was centralisation from above should be seen as a measure of the weakness of the Italian agrarian and industrial bourgeoisie which had been the driving force behind Unification and its inability to impose cultural and political hegemony over society as a whole.

Thus in place of the Farini-Minghetti bill the Government passed a Law in 1865 (Law N. 2248) which introduced a rigid prefectorial system along Napoleonic lines. The prefect became the representative of executive power at local and provincial level with wide-ranging authority over numerous spheres of influence, including education, law and order, administration and justice.

2.1.2 Establishing the regions
It was not until the end of the Second World War that administrative decentralisation was once again seriously considered. One of the reasons for this

was a general agreement that Fascism's rise to power had been made easier by the centralistic character of the Italian Liberal State. A more balanced division of power would prevent the recurrence of an authoritarian solution. Another powerful motive-force was the climate of reforms prevalent after the war, which led to a widespread consensus that the reconstruction of the Italian political system ought to take place along new democratic lines and not be remodelled around pre-fascist Liberal institutions.

Despite these common aspirations of the anti-fascist parties, there was no clear convergence on the question of regional autonomy. The Socialist and Communist Parties, in particular, were suspicious of any form of federalism in case it promoted reactionary political tendencies at the periphery: the left-wing parties in this respect showed only limited appreciation of the innovative potential of a regional political system (Ragionieri, 1976, p. 2481).

The end-result was that the Italian Constitution, elaborated in 1947 and formally introduced on 1 January 1948, established the regions as administrative entities with limited legislative powers in a number of fields, including police, health services, town planning, tourism, local transport and communications, public works, agriculture and forestry. The regions were denied 'primary' legislative responsibility, i.e. the authority to legislate independently of the State and were attributed only 'concurrent' and 'subsidiary' legislative responsibility, in other words the authority to formulate legislative initiatives complementary to or within the framework of national legislation. The 1948 Constitution provided for the establishment of twenty regions, of which five were to enjoy 'special autonomy' (or 'Statute', equivalent to a region's constitution) and the remaining fifteen 'ordinary autonomy' (or Statute).

In this, as in other fields, the Italian Constitution was not applied for several years. The Statutes of four of the five special regions (Sicily, Sardinia, Valle d'Aosta and Trentino Alto Adige) were approved in February 1948; the fifth special region, Friuli-Venezia Giulia, was established in 1963. There were specific political reasons why these regions received favourable treatment, namely the fact that they included considerable ethnic minorities (the three northern ones) or had shown separatist tendencies (Sicily and Sardinia).

The 'ordinary' regions had to wait until the 1970s, despite the left-wing parties' change of heart vis-à-vis decentralisation after they were ousted from government in 1947 and after their defeat in the general elections of 1948. The Christian Democratic Party (*Democrazia Cristiana*, or DC) was in power and had no intention of strengthening the Communist Party (*Partito Comunista*, or PCI) in the latter's regional strongholds in Central Italy. Nor were there strong demands for decentralisation coming from Italian society. According to Nanetti, 'it was a society with a small number of élites whose economic and political interests were served well by centralised institutional decision-making [...]. These demands [for regional government] had to wait for the political events and economic and social changes of the 1960s' (Nanetti, 1988, p. 80).

Thanks to these changes, above all the development of an increasingly pluralistic society with the emergence of new social and interest groups accompanied by the political success of the Left parties, pressure mounted in the country for breaking the Christian Democrats' monopoly of political power and for a degree of power-sharing. The creation of the regions in 1972 was granted by the then Prime Minister, Andreotti, in response to this new social and political pressure. Great hopes were held at the time regarding the regenerating effect administrative decentralisation would have upon the Italian system of government, which by then had shown itself unable to implement radical reforms in line with the country's rapid industrialisation. Yet cautionary notes were raised from various quarters. Earle summed up the various reactions to the regional experiment at the beginning of the 1970s as follows: 'At best it can inject new vigour and more direct democracy into the machinery of government, acting as a vehicle for progress and enrichment of life at all levels. At worst, it can insert a parasitic layer of maladministration between the central government and the ninety-four provinces, adding to the opportunity for *clientelismo*, intrigue and corruption' (Earle, 1974, p. 90). As we shall see, both forecasts turned out to be correct.

2.1.3. The Regions since 1970

A series of laws were passed in the 1970s to set up the regional system. The 1972 decrees followed the 1970 regional elections granting the regions limited powers. Law 382 of 1975 gave the regions wide-ranging powers within the scope of the Constitution (no primary legislative authority therefore). The 616 decrees in 1977 'institutionalised the regions as real centres of policy-making' (Nanetti, 1988, p. 81). The decrees gave the regions control over 25% of the entire national budget (Putnam, Leonardi and Nanetti, 1985, p. 80). It should be noted, however, that according to Art. 119 of the Constitution the regions enjoy 'financial autonomy in the forms and within the limits prescribed by the Republic's laws which co-ordinate it with the finance of the State, Provinces and Communes'. The prevalent interpretation of Art. 119 has always been that the financial autonomy of the fifteen ordinary regions is very limited, as they cannot impose new taxes or regulate the imposition or distribution of taxes which are already in place. Thus the 'financial autonomy' attributed to the regions by Art. 119 consists mainly in the autonomy to administer directly their income as fixed by the State. Greater financial autonomy is attributed to the five regions with special Statute, although only in exceptional cases do they have the power to impose their own taxes.

As for regional government, Art. 121 of the Constitution states that 'the organs of the Regions are the Council, the Junta and the President', whose functions correspond roughly to those of Parliament, the Government and the President of the Republic. The council is made up of between 30 and 80 councillors and has legislative, regulating and administrative responsibilities, as well as functions of political control over the junta and the president and also over the region's policy-making. The junta is the executive body and is elected by council, whereas the president, also elected by council, is both the region's representative and the president of the junta. Councils approve the regions' Statutes, which require an absolute majority and have to be approved by Parliament by law. The Statutes regulate the internal organisation of the region, including the composition of the junta and the system for electing the junta and its president. They also regulate relations between the different regional government bodies and their functions. Regional Statutes, however, cannot regulate or modify the type or number of regional Government bodies, the functions of such bodies, the electoral system for councillors or the widening of a region's territory. Statutes also contain regulations concerning popular legislative initiatives and regional referenda.

Below the regions, administrative decentralisation rests with the provinces and the communes. The provinces, after the creation of the regions, became rather hybrid institutions, since many of their powers were lost. Many experts advocated the abolition of the provinces but a recent Law, passed in 1991, retained them as administrative entities (see below). The communes are the only territorial bodies to pre-date Italy's Unification and indeed the Constitution simply granted them official recognition, as opposed to creating them *ex novo*.

Since the establishment of the regions, the two main areas of contention and ambiguity have been precisely the relation between and respective spheres of influence of the regions and the State on the one hand and the regions and the other tiers of local government (provinces and communes) on the other (Cammelli, 1990). As far as the regions and the State are concerned, the main limitation to the autonomy of the former is the Government's power to contest the constitutionality of a regional law. The Government can invite the regional council to reconsider any law this has passed; such a law can be re-approved by council, provided it is approved by an absolute rather than a simple majority of councillors. After that, central government has fifteen days in which to appeal to the Constitutional Court. Conversely, the regions themselves can resort to the Court against the State if in their opinion it violates their functions.

There have been numerous cases brought to the attention of the Constitutional Court since the regions started to operate. The Court's initial tendency was to rule in favour of the State thus in the 1970s the prevalent attitude on the part of the regions was to find a compromise with the State and avoid recourse to the Court for fear of this body's anti-regional orientation. (Rodotà, 1986, p. 91). In the 1980s the attitude of the Court towards the regions became much more positive. In the same decade, regional autonomy vis-à-vis the State increased considerably so that this aspect can no longer be treated as a central issue; rather, it has been replaced by a struggle between regional and local government (Putnam, 1993, p. 46).

Have the regions found popular favour? Have they commanded attention and established roots? These questions need to be considered alongside the question of the performance of the regions, which also achieved new prominence since the overcoming of the main problem posed by State-regions relations. Both the above questions, i.e. popular affection/disaffection towards the regions and regional performance, are closely linked, since new institutions need to have a positive impact upon the society in which they operate in order to establish roots and command popular support.

According to Hine, the performance of all regions has been disappointing in so far as they have become an integral part of the Italian political system and are in themselves entrenched in 'partyocracy'. 'The parties act as channels through which regions and regional party leaders can bring pressures on the centre' (Hine, 1993, p. 271). Despite their limited financial autonomy, for example, the regions operated large deficits in the 1980s in the knowledge that the centre - and the national taxpayers - would bail them out, which regularly happened. From this point of view the pessimistic forecast that the regions would add another layer to the clientelistic Italian body politic can be deemed to have been correct. The recent Italian scandal known as '*Tangentopoli*', from the word '*tangente*' meaning a cut paid by private and public companies to political parties in exchange for public contracts and favourable treatment, has involved many local and regional executives throughout Italy. The scandal was uncovered in Milan but it soon spread to other parts of Italy, involving all the main political parties, above all the Christian Democrats and the Socialists (*Partito Socialista*, or PSI). Whereas scandals of this type had previously often been associated with party politics and State intervention in the South, *Tangentopoli* seemed to have unified all Italy on the basis of maladministration. Yet this may well turn out to be a rather superficial picture.

Beyond and above the clientelistic aspect typical until recently of Italian politics at all levels, it is possible to distinguish between two different groups of regions in terms both of performance and popular esteem. Various studies have brought to light the consistently better performance of the Central and Northern regions vis-à-vis the Southern ones (Leonardi, Nanetti and Putnam, 1985; Putnam, 1993). The perceptions of the performance of local and regional government on the part of Italians vary sharply, accurately reflecting this geographical division. Northern and Central Italians are generally satisfied with their local and regional governments whereas they express dissatisfaction for central government; by contrast, Southern Italians are dissatisfied with all tiers of government, judged to be inefficient, ineffective and corrupt (Putnam, 1993, pp. 54-6). The reasons for this are varied and have been traced back to different levels of economic development, uneven distribution of resources, historical traditions and, more recently, different degrees of 'civic-ness', measured in terms of active participation in democratic and political associations, trust and solidarity, community values and political equality (Putnam, 1993, p. 86-120).

As these issues concern the social and political cultures of different regions of Italy, rather than the regional system *per se* and bring back to prominence the Italian 'Southern Question', they will be discussed in some detail below, together with the new regionalist political movements and approaches to regional policy and regional development.

2.2 Regionalism as a political movement and current of thought
2.2.1 The Federalist movement at the time of Unification.
Strictly speaking, one cannot speak of a federal political movement at the time of Unification. The two great political leaders of the Italian *Risorgimento*, Cavour and Mazzini, were both anti-federalist, although they were in favour of some measure of devolution of power. There were, however, various federalist thinkers who were in varying degrees influential among the political and cultural élite, despite lacking popular following. Among these one should mention Carlo Cattaneo (1801-1869) and Giuseppe Ferrari (1811-1876), both from Lombardy. The former was a radical Liberal who believed that individual freedom came before nationalism and the respect of local/regional diversities before the need for a strong, centralised State. Before 1848 Cattaneo was ready to accept autonomous rule for Lombardy within a federal Austrian Empire (Mack Smith, 1968, p. 92) and even after that date he was more concerned with the abolition of trade barriers between the various Italian regional States than with national unity. Cattaneo was not a political leader and his influence on Italian society and politics remained limited, although in Lombardy itself he was a popular figure. Likewise, Ferrari was an intellectual and philosopher who remained at the margins of active politics. He, too, advocated a federal Italy, on the grounds that 'our history rejects the possibility or desirability of our becoming a unitary nation; on the other hand a federal system will enable us to reach the very highest goals [...]. We may regard federalism as the purest form of constitutional government, founding liberty on a written pact, on a multiplicity of assemblies,

on the inviolability of all internal frontiers, and the solemnity of its central parliament' (Speech to Parliament, 8 October 1860).

Vincenzo Gioberti (1801-1852), a Piedmontese, advocated a federal union sponsored by the Pope, a project which collapsed when Pope Pius IX turned against Liberalism and the cause for National Unification after the 1848-49 revolutions. Gioberti had a clear vision of the fact that an Italian people did not exist and needed to be created taking into account existing divisions in 'government, laws, institutions, popular folklore, customs, sentiment and habits'. To this end he judged the creation of a single unitary State to be either madness or, if brought about by force, an immoral crime.

As Donzelli (1992, p. 6) pointed out, the federalist current of thought that can be traced back to the Italian *Risorgimento* tradition can be defined as 'instrumental in ascent', that is to say, a federalism which identifies strong ethnic, linguistic, social and cultural differences within a territory seen as capable of achieving national unity. The federal system is seen in this context as a transitory system, an instrument to bring about the 'harmonisation' and real unification of a State's regional components.

2.2.2 The New Federalism

Today's federalism - the federalism of the Italian Northern League Party (*Lega Nord*)- differs fundamentally from that of the *Risorgimento* and can be defined (Donzelli, 1992, p. 6) as 'instrumental in descent', despite the League's protestations that they are Cattaneo's natural heirs. By this expression Donzelli refers to the League's secessionist aspirations and its openly-held convinction that Northern and Southern Italy represent two distinct and non-converging societies which ought to be free to go it alone. The League's position presupposes the total rejection of the Italian Fathers' aspirations to achieve complete unity through the creation of a common people.

Paradoxically, the revival of federalist/ethnic sentiments has taken place at a time when Italy has reached a high degree of cultural homogeneity, not least from a linguistic point of view. Apart from minority ethnic groups, linguistic unification is now an accomplished reality. Census results indicate that Italian is now prevailing, although the dialects have not disappeared. Most people can speak both Italian and a dialect, and the percentage of people who speak only or mainly Italian is constantly growing (Lepschy and Lepschy, 1991; Lepschy, Lepschy and Voghera, 1993).

The Northern League strongly defends the use of the dialect and has provocatively asked for the 'Lombard' dialect to be used as official language. Yet it was not linguistic 'nostalgia' that provided the stimulus for the new federalism. Rather, it was the deterioration of political institutions, the growth of organised crime, and the systematic use of corrupt practices in business transactions involving party and State officials unearthed by the recent '*Tangentopoli*' scandal. In the eyes of the League the 'Southernisation' of the Italian State as evidenced by the emergence of a widespread corrupt and clientelistic system of government is a clear sign that the process of national unification, far from promoting the homogeneisation of the country around 'Northern' laws, practices, institutions and economy, has succeeded only in imposing 'Southern' deviant practices upon the whole of the country.

In addition, socio-economic development remains uneven. The North/South divide is, as we shall see, still highly relevant, but there are also differences between the other regions. Back in the 1970s Bagnasco (1977) identified 'three Italies' in terms of social and economic structures: the industrial, urban-centred and large-firms-dominated North-West; the newly developed, still semi-rural, small-firms-dominated North-Eastern and Central regions; and the under-developed South. Since then much important research has been produced attempting to explain the reasons behind as well as the characteristics of each area (or model) of development.

The federalism of the League, as put forward in the party's 1992 electoral programme, appears to have been rather crudely inspired by the findings of Bagnasco and other sociologists. The League advocated the creation of a Federal State made up of three macro-regions or Republics (North, Centre and South), each considered as homogeneous from a socio-economic point of view. The Federal State would be responsible only for foreign affairs, defence, justice, general finance and higher education. The emphasis was on the creation of a Northern Republic made up of Lombardy, Piedmont, Venetia, Liguria, Emilia-Romagna and Tuscany, represented in the party literature as the most socially advanced part of Italy, governed and 'oppressed' by the Southern-dominated State bureaucracy and party system.

The starting point for setting up the three macro-regions – or at any rate the Northern one which was the one that really mattered for the League – was, according to the party, a formally legal and constitutional procedure. Art. 132 of the Constitution states that it is legitimate to provide for the fusion of existing Regions by Constitutional Law, as long as this is requested by a number of Municipal Councils representing at least a third of the interested population, and provided that the proposal is approved in a referendum by a majority of the same population.

The Northern League was considered in the late 1980s a fringe protest movement, with an extreme populistic political programme which would fail to make inroads into the more educated and middle-class electorate. However, this prediction turned out to be wrong. The party obtained good electoral results in the Northern provinces, particularly in Lombardy, at the 1990 administrative elections, did surprisingly well in the 1992 general political elections and won across the Northern regions in the 1993 local and provincial elections, gaining Milan as well as scores of minor wealthy industrial towns.

The collapse of the Socialist and Christian Democratic parties following the *Tangentopoli* scandal appears to have created a new division in the country in terms of political behaviour, with the possible consequence of a more drastic political split. As the federalism of the 1990s brings us back once again to the question of the North/South divide, I will discuss it in greater depth below.

2.3 Regional policy and regional development

The Italian Regional Question centres around the under-development of the South, and both regional policy and regional development schemes have been dominated by the need to solve this basic North/South divide. The first serious attempt to promote economic and social development in the region occurred in the first decade of the twentieth century, when successive Italian Governments, headed by Giuseppe Zanardelli first and Giovanni Giolitti later, prepared a series of laws designed for a few Southern regions. At that time Italy had begun to industrialise (the country's first industrial take-off is deemed to have occurred between 1896 and 1913). Provision was made for measures of agricultural improvement, public works and health schemes. As for industrial development, the city of Naples was designated as an industrial growth area and a new steel plant was set up in one of its suburbs. The policy largely failed, partly due to the absence of an indigenous entrepreneurial culture but above all, according to Clark, to a lack of resources as well as corruption: 'here are the beginnings of constant themes in twentieth-century Italian politics: the distribution in the South of subsidies and patronage by central State development agencies, and the use of such agencies to win political support' (Clark, 1983, p. 133).

In the 1950s the Italian State made a much more decisive attempt to develop the Southern economy. In August 1950 the Law establishing the *Cassa per Opere Straordinarie di Pubblico Interesse nell'Italia Meridionale*, better known as the *Cassa per il Mezzogiorno*, was passed. The function of the *Cassa* was clear from its title, namely to undertake 'extraordinary interventions' over and above what normal government Ministries could achieve. In the intentions of the legislators the *Cassa* was to be a public body with its own legal status, largely independent of the civil service. Yet it was made responsible to the Minister for the *Mezzogiorno* and subject to government control. The *Cassa's* efforts to develop the South can be divided into three main phases: 1950-57 when the emphasis was on modernising agriculture and building infrastructure related primarily to agriculture; 1957-71 when industry was singled out (Law 634 of 1957) as the sector that needed to receive greatest attention; 1971-84, i.e., the post-'heavy industry' and recession years.

The first phase was marked, as well as by the creation of the *Cassa*, by the land reform laws of 1950: *Legge Sila* in May, *Legge Stralcio* in October and *Legge Siciliana* in December. These laws were aimed at reducing the power and the size of the estates of the large absentee landowners (*latifondisti*). Part of their land was expropriated and sub-divided into small plots of land which were assigned to landless labourers or petty landowners. The farming plots thus created had the short-term effect of reducing the chronic unemployment and under-employment of the area and easing social tensions, as well as stealing the thunder of the Communist Party, which had backed the Southern peasants' agitations of the 1940s and received growing political support from them in return. The policy of favouring the peasant farm model, however, was not economically viable and when Italy joined the European Community the backward state of Southern agriculture became even more evident. Emigration to the North at the time of the country's economic miracle also drained human resources from the Southern countryside and resulted in the abandonment of many of the newly created family farms.

The shift in regional policy from promoting agriculture to promoting industrial development was thus inevitable. What kind of industries should be promoted became a key issue. An important objective of regional development was to encourage the formation of small and medium-sized firms and the emergence of indigenous entrepreneurship. In reality, however, the Italian State had to rely on the public sector, mainly the two giant State holding companies IRI and ENI, to make investments in the South, with the consequence that many industrial plants set up in the Southern regions were in the capital-intensive, 'heavy' industrial sector, whose success turned out to be deeply conditioned by external events. With the energy crisis of the early 1970s and steel over-production throughout Europe the fate of these plants became highly uncertain. Furthermore, there were few 'trickle-down' effects upon the local/

regional economy and these large plants' failure to stimulate the growth of small and medium-sized firms earned them their famous nickname 'cathedrals in the desert'.

Lack of co-ordination and planning, excessive bureaucracy and sheer corruption were blamed in the 1970s for the poor results achieved by the *Cassa*. Excessive centralisation was another factor judged as having a negative effect on Southern development. After the creation of the regions in the 1970s pressure mounted for delegating some or all of the powers of the Central Agency to the regions; indeed in the late seventies there were increasing demands for the suppression of the *Cassa*. The Cassa was finally abolished in 1984, and in 1986 Law 64 gave extraordinary powers to the regions in what constituted another major policy shift. It was felt that if regional governments were left to formulate and implement their own plans, intervention would be far more effective as the regions were more familiar with local conditions, needs and resources.

One of the main problems identified with the functioning of the *Cassa* was the gap between legislation and its transmission and translation into action. This has been largely explained on the basis that the *Cassa* was used to fulfil a political function: local Christian Democrat leaders systematically plundered resources to give their party a strong power base (Chubb, 1990). In this context it mattered little whether the plans were actually implemented, so long as money continued to sustain the party's own clienteles. In the 1980s the Socialist Party exercised a similar role.

Law 64 of 1986 has recently been subjected to intense scrutiny and it has incurred severe criticism. The regional governments have proved largely incapable of drawing up - let alone implement - development projects themselves, and the usual problems of clientelism and corruption are still apparent, this time on a regional level. Given what was said under 2.1.3 above, regarding the maladministration of the Southern regions, regional policy and regional development have not yet found their best administrative/political framework.

Today, despite the ever-present gap between North and South, it is the very concept of regional development which is being put into question. This is partly due to the fact that the failure to develop the South in the past decades has led many Northerners to doubt the wisdom of subsidising the South (Becchi, 1992). Less 'noble' motives include fiscal pressure (harsher in the North), the immense Government deficit and the economic recession which has hit Northern industry.

A study promoted by the Regional Council of the Veneto Region shows that between 1985 and 1990 four Northern regions, Lombardy, Piedmont, Veneto and Emilia-Romagna paid 45% of national taxes, 62% of VAT, and 63.5% of local taxes. They were given by the State 33.9% of the funds redistributed to local and regional governments. Thus for every 100 Lire paid to the State the Lombards received back for their own use 24.5, the Piedmontese 30, the Venetians 35 and the Emilians 37. By contrast, Molise could spend 80, Campania 64, Puglia 58, Calabria 84 and Basilicata 85 (*La Repubblica*, 1 April 1992, p. 14). The Southern regions depend on government financing and 'are terrified that the Government may ultimately expect them to depend on their own resources and taxes instead of giving them lavish subsidies' (Haycraft, 1985, p. 19). As Hine explains, in Italy's present regional system the coalition between the Ministry of Finance and the Southern regions has numerical superiority over the Northern regions, which are often politically divided among themselves. The new federalism advocated by the Northern League must thus be viewed in the context of this increasing frustration and sense of impotence on the part of the richest half of the country.

3. Italian regionalism today
3.1 The evolution of decentralisation
In June 1990 a new Law on local government (Law N. 142) was passed, with two primary objectives. The first objective was to reduce clientelism and encourage local governments' accountability to their electors, mainly through greater participation by ordinary citizens (*via* referenda, petitions or proposals - Art. 6), access to information (Art. 7) and the creation of a '*difensore civico*' or guarantor of impartiality and good administration (Art. 8). The second objective was to regulate relations between the three tiers of government, central, regional and local. Greater importance was attributed to the regions in this tri-partite relationship compared to that allowed for by Articles 117 and 118 of the Constitution. Whereas these articles stated that 'Provinces and Communes are autonomous bodies within the context of the principles established by the laws of the Republic which determine their functions', Art. 3 of Law 142 elevates the regions to a position of superiority vis-à-vis the provinces and communes in terms of socio-economic and territorial planning. The regions are assigned the important functions of determining general policy objectives, although local and provincial governments contribute to their formulation. Law 142 is, in this respect, ambiguous since it does not clarify in what ways and on the basis of which criteria communes and provinces contribute to general policy planning.

Despite the wider functions attributed to the regions by the new Law, they are far from being satisfied. The rise of the Northern League Party, and the (until recently) extreme form of federalism it advocated, provided the regions with both new ammunition and a new sense of urgency. On 19 December 1990 the regional council of one of the regions with special Statute, Friuli-Venezia Giulia, approved, with the support of the Christian Democrats, Socialists, Communists and Greens, an agenda for a federalist reform of the Italian State. A similar request was put forward by Trentino-Alto Adige on 19 February 1991. On 8 March it was the turn of another 'special' region, Valle D'Aosta. On 26 February 1991 one of the 'ordinary' regions, the wealthy Northern Emilia-Romagna, requested a new type of regionalism. The main target of all the above regions was Art. 117 of the Constitution, which limits the functions of the regions.

The Northern regions' demand for a federal State has as its model the German division into *Länder*, with the central State left with a co-ordinating role and the regions entitled to financial autonomy and full powers of intervention in all sectors within their territories. The central State would be left with international relations, national defence, justice and monetary policy. The Northern regions' proposals for a Federal State reject the division of Italy into three macro-regions (virtually three separate States) which characterises the political programme of the Northern League and in particular that party's provocative suggestion that the North should form its own Republic, fully integrated within the EC, leaving the rest of Italy to its own destiny. Yet the League itself has shifted position in recent times. If there is a convergence between the strategy of the Northern League (and perhaps even of the Democratic Party of the Left, i.e., the offspring of the old *Partito Comunista*) and the Northern regions' aspirations to greater political and financial autonomy, we can expect regionalism in Italy to gain an almost unstoppable momentum.

3.2. Regionalism as a political force

I have already emphasised the growing success of the Northern League at recent political and administrative elections. The rise of this new party to a dominant position in the north of the country has been accompanied by its increasing efforts to appeal to the middle classes and become less associated with extreme political views, including secessionism. Whereas Miglio, the ideologue of the party, appears to remain firm in advocating the creation of three macro-regions on the basis of economic and social homogeneity, the powerful leader of the League, Umberto Bossi, proposed in April 1993 changing the name of his party from Northern League to Federal Italy League, implying that he now accepted the unitary State created by the *Risorgimento* and no longer advocated a process of political dismemberment of the Italian peninsula.

The mood of the Italian people, meanwhile, appears to have turned decisively in favour of the regions, if only in protest against the maladministration of central government. On 18 April 1993 Italians were asked to vote in eight referenda, two of which were sponsored by the regions. One of these concerned the abolition of the Ministry of Agriculture, the other the abolition of the Ministry of Tourism; in both cases the functions of the Ministries were to pass to the regions. Both referenda were approved by a majority of Italians.

A third referendum was to determine whether Italians wished to extend to all towns the majority system which assigns two-thirds of the seats to the winning list and to elect the mayor directly in municipal elections. This referendum was also approved, together with a fourth which established that 238 Senators out of 315 were to be elected with a majority system and only 77 with the system of proportional representation established in Italy after the fall of Fascism. These last two referenda represented the clearest indication yet of the will of the Italians to change their electoral and political system at the roots and to create their 'Second Republic'.

The political situation in Italy is at present evolving so rapidly that it is almost impossible to predict how the country's political institutions will be reformed, including the regional system. In the administrative elections of June 1993 the picture that emerged was of an Italy divided politically into three, the North dominated by the Northern League (with the exception of Emilia-Romagna), the Centre by the PDS (the Democratic Party of the Left, i.e. the former Communists), and the South governed by heterogeneous coalitions, generally made up of anti-Mafia and anti-Camorra alliances, although in some cases the vote-controlling criminal/clientelistic machinery survived almost unscathed.

More recently, at the March 1994 elections, two new parties emerged which put national unity and even nationalism back on the political agenda: *Forza Italia*, led by the media tycoon Silvio Berlusconi, and *Alleanza Nazionale*, made up largely of the neo-fascists (or ex-fascists as they prefer to be considered). Geographical divisions have not disappeared, however, since the Northern League remained strong in the northern regions and Alleanza Nazionale was primarily successful in the south. At present the new Italian government is made up of an uneasy coalition between these three parties.

3.3. What future for regional development?

Whether the more extreme or the more moderate form of federalism (or simply a more substantial devolution of power to the regions) will prevail, the Italian regional divide is clearly there to stay. The question is, will a federal State or a more radical form of regionalism promote or hinder the cause of national harmonisation? Would it simply represent the triumph of the new 'selfishness' of the richest regions, or could it also be considered as a step forward for the least developed ones?

More than forty years of regional policy and regional development have left the south at best modernised but certainly not developed. There now seems to be a growing consensus that there must be an end to indiscriminate subsidies and politically-motivated, centrally-controlled transfers of money from the Northern to the Southern regions. The League's solution would be a neo-Liberal one, where incentives to development should consist of lower wages (justified on the basis of an alleged lower cost of living in the south), tax incentives for businesses on the basis of strictly documented profits on their part, and an end to all State subsidies. At times the League seems to accept the concept of a transfer of funds, provided this takes place directly from the Northern to the Southern regions under the control of the former as opposed to that of the State.

The traditional parties are more oriented towards the preservation of some forms of direct subsidies, but with more rigorous methods of control. The two new parties which emphasise national unity, *Forza Italia* and *Alleanze Nazionale*, have not spelt out a clear policy for the south. Now that they are in Government the temptation to resort to a renewed version of clientelism is no doubt strong, particularly in the case of *Alleanza Nazionale* which depends to a very large extent on a southern electorate. As things stand at present it is extremely difficult to predict whether the Northern League will be able to impose its own neo-liberal policies or whether the south will be tied to central government via clientelism and patronage as so often in the past.

4. Italian regionalism within the context of Europe

Italy was a founder member of the European Community and the Italian population has consistently showed firm support for European integration (Hine, 1993, p. 286). European unity is not a political issue in the country; if anything, the recently formed Northern League is even more pro-European than the traditional parties. This is due to the fact that they believe that a Europe of regions will eventually supplant the existing Europe of nation-states and thus allow Northern Italy to rejoin its transalpine neighbours.

As Umberto Bossi stated in his autobiography: 'What is the meaning of having frontiers between Piedmont and Savoie, or South Tyrol and Austria? Their ethnicity is substantially identical, from a naturalistic point of view. From a socio-cultural point of view [...] nothing unites Trentino or Lombardy with Calabria or Campania. Therefore I say: why not replace the fixed frontiers and the centralism typical of unitary States with a more articulated system, characterised by a plurality of institutional centres each with specific and limited responsibilities? Why not eliminate, in other words, the rigid frontiers between very similar realities, as for example Lombardy and Baviera, while introducing separate decision-making centres, each with real autonomy, in different realities which were arbitrarily unified, such as the North and South of Italy?' (Bossi, 1992, pp. 161-62).

The advocation of a return of northern Italy to its 'natural' Mitteleuropean cradle could not have been more openly and clearly stated. As with the League's other political proposals, such ideals reflect the complete failure, in their eyes, of the Italian nation-state. European integration is viewed in this context as little more than an opportunity to achieve the party's secessionist goal. As the Northern League becomes less extreme in its political views, we can expect their appreciation of European integration to change accordingly.

However, the need to abolish political, as well as trade barriers between regions which are homogeneous from a socio-economic point of view and which have already established close economic ties, is widely understood by other political actors, not least the regions themselves. The internationalisation of economic markets and the creation, in particular, of the Single European Market have had the effect of encouraging transnational inter-firm (and in many cases inter-regional) collaborative agreements. France, particularly the Rhône-Alpes Region, has become a favourite place for Italian firms to invest in, partly because of its perceived cultural and political affinity. Many Piedmontese and Lombard firms have established subsidiaries in France, often making use of the French Government's incentives for attracting foreign investment to underdeveloped areas, such as Haute Savoie.

With economic ties across Europe becoming stronger, the idea of a federal Europe may acquire a new legitimacy. Indeed, the Maastricht Treaty contains clauses which hint at the possible establishment of a Federal Europe of the Regions. Yet a federal solution is at present not at all popular with most European peoples, as poll after poll have shown. Italy in this respect may well represent the odd man out, although one suspects that the pro-Europeanism of most Italians has little to do with perceived inter-regional and trans-national social and economic homogeneity and a lot to do with a distrust of central Government, i.e., the same distrust which has turned Italians into supporters of a radical new form of regionalism. As *The Economist* recently pointed out: 'Italy was an enthusiastic signatory of the Maastricht Treaty in December 1991, not just because it has always been Europhilic but because the Maastricht requirements of economic and monetary convergence would impose the discipline that Italy's governments normally fail to find on their own [...] What will happen now, if the Maastricht process becomes more fuzzy? The answer is that Italians will have to rely on their own politicians, not anyone else's' (*The Economist*, 26 June 1993, p. 21).

A radical and effective reform of the country's political system and the establishment of a strong and authoritative executive may yet re-establish the credibility of the Italian nation-state in the eyes of its citizens. This is no doubt one of the aspirations of Berlusconi's *Forza Italia* and it is not a coincidence that this party is more tepid towards Europe than either the traditional parties or the Northern League. Just as the mood of Italians appears to be oscillating between an extreme form of regionalism and revived nationalism, so the country's attitude towards Europe and its assessment of the merits of a federal, as opposed to a confederal, Europe seem to suffer from a general state of fickleness.

References

Bagnasco, A. (1977), *Tre Italie. La problematica territoriale dello sviluppo italiano*, Bologna, Il Mulino.

Becchi, A. (1992), 'Incentivi statali, pesante eredità', in *A sud di qualunque nord*, Il Manifesto del mese, n. 8.

Bossi, U. (with D. Vimercati) (1992), *Vento dal Nord. La mia Lega la mia vita*, Milan, Sperling and Kupfer.

Cammelli, M. 'Regioni e rappresentanza degli interessi: il caso italiano', *Stato e mercato*, N. 2. August 1990, pp. 151-200.

Chubb, J. (1990), Patronage, power and poverty in Southern Italy, Cambridge, Cambridge University Press.

Clark, M. (1983), *Modern Italy 1871-1982*, London and New York, Longman.

De Mauro, T. (1963), *Storia linguistica dell'Italia unita*, Bari, Laterza.

Delpino, L. and F. Del Giudice (1992), *Diritto amministrativo*, Naples, Simone.

Donzelli, C. (1992), 'Le oscillazioni del federalismo', in *A sud di qualunque nord*, Il Manifesto del mese, n.8.

Earle, J. (1974), *Italy in the 1970s*, Newton Abbot and Vancouver, David and Charles.

Falzone, V., F. Palermo, and F. Cosentino (eds.) (1976), *La Costituzione della Repubblica Italiana. Illustrata con i lavori preparatori*, Milan, Mondadori.

Haycraft, J. (1985), *Italian Labyrinth*, Harmondsworth, Penguin.

Hine, D. (1993), *Governing Italy. The politics of Bargained Pluralism*, Oxford, Clarendon Press.

Italia, V. and M. Bassani (eds.) (1990), *Le autonomie locali. Legge 8 giugno 1990, n. 142)*, Milan, Giuffrè.

La Repubblica, 1 April 1992.

Lega Lombarda-Lega Nord, *Programma elettorale*, February 1992.

Lepschy, A.L. and G. Lepschy (1991), *The Italian Language Today*, London, Routledge.

Lepschy, A.L., G. Lepschy and M. Voghera, M. (1993), 'Linguistic Variety in Italy', paper given at the 1992 Annual Conference of the Association for the Study of Modern Italy [ASMI]. A summary of this paper appeared in the ASMI Newsletter, N. 23, Spring 1993.

Mack Smith, D. (1985), *Cavour*, London, Methuen.

Mack Smith, D. (ed.) (1968), *The Making of Italy*, New York, Harper and Row.

Nanetti, R. (1988), *Growth and Territorial Policies. The Italian Model of Social Capitalism*, London and New York, Pinter.

Putnam, R. D. (with R. Leonardi and R. Nanetti) (1993), *Making Democracy Work. Civic Traditions in Modern Italy*, Princeton, New Jersey, Princeton University Press.

Putnam, R. D., R. Leonardi and R. Nanetti (1985), *La pianta e le radici*, Bologna, Il Mulino.

Ragionieri, E. (1976), *La storia politica e sociale*, Storia d'Italia, Vol 4:3, Turin, Einaudi.

Rodotà, C. (1986), *La Corte Costituzionale*, Rome, Editori Riuniti.

Rupeni, A. (ed.) (1980), *Comuni e Province negli anni 80*, Rome, Cinque Lune.

The Economist, 26 June 1993.

The following place labels appear on the map:

AZORES (Portugal)
0 km 100

MADEIRA (Portugal)
0 km 100

0 100 200
kilometres

Bay of Biscay

FRANCE

Ovideo•
ASTURIAS
CANTABRIA
BASQUE COUNTRY
NAVARRA
ANDORRA

• Santiago
GALICIA

CASTILLA-LEON
RIOJA

• Zaragoza
CATALONIA
Barcelona •

NORTH
• Valladolid
ARAGON

• Oporto

PORTUGAL

MADRID
■ Madrid

CENTRAL

BALEARIC ISLANDS
Palma •

LISBON
• Lisbon

EXTREMADURA

• Toledo
CASTILLA-LA MANCHA

Valencia
Gulf of Valencia

SPAIN

• Mérida

COMUNIDAD VALENCIANA

ALENTEJO

Murcia •
MURCIA

ALGARVE

Seville •
ANDALUSIA

Mediterranean Sea

Gulf of Cadiz

ALGERIA

Gibraltar (BR.)
Strait of Gibraltar
CEUTA (SP.)

CANARY ISLANDS (SP.)

MELILLA (SP.)
0 km 100

MOROCCO

Regionalism in Iberia
Allan Williams

1. Introduction: Cultural roots, uneven economic development and political centralisation

The two Iberian neighbours have had sharply divergent experiences of regionalism and nationalism. Portugal is one of the most unified nation-states in Europe and, apart from some separatist rumblings in the Atlantic islands, the legitimacy of the Portuguese state has not been questioned seriously by any of its regions in more than half a millennium. In contrast, Spain today has a Constitution which enshrines the rights of its regions. It also has experienced, and continues to experience, substantial democratic and violent challenges in some regions to the form and the very existence of the state. This itself is the culmination of four major phases of separatist movements since the beginning of the nineteenth century (Newton, 1983, p. 98): the *junta* movement during the Peninsular War; *cantonalismo* in the 1870s after the overthrow of Isabella II; nationalist movements in the early twentieth century following the break down of the Restoration Regime; and the democratic Republican movement in the 1930s.

In the latter years of the Franco regime, regionalism and nationalism became intertwined with the democratic opposition movements, and this contributed to the priority given to the regional question in the post-Franco political settlement. But despite - or perhaps because of - the 1978 Constitution which recognised the *España de Las Autonomías*, it is possible to agree with Guerra's (1989, p. 19) view that national and regional diversity is 'without doubt the greatest political problem which the still young Spanish democracy faces today'. In Portugal, in contrast, the post-1974 democratic transition was in many ways far more dramatic, with tanks on the streets and attempted counter-coups. However, it was also unconstrained by the dictates of nationalism and regionalism. In the remainder of this opening section, we consider the bases - or the lack of these - for regionalism and nationalism in Iberia.

Spain has a long and relatively early history of state formation. During the reconquest from the Moors a number of independent Christian kingdoms were formed which were unified after the marriage of Isabella and Ferdinand in the fifteenth century. However, centralisation was limited for outside of Castille traditional rights, privileges and laws were respected. As a result, Spain could best be described as 'a confederation of political units' (Tamames and Clegg, 1984, p. 32). Under the Bourbons, these traditional rights were reduced during the eighteenth century but, even so, the Basque Country retained its ancient rights - the *fueros* - until the twentieth century. Political centralisation did not, however, lead to a unified nation-state. Regionalist pressures re-emerged in the late nineteenth century, partly due to the impact of uneven development which widened the differences between the economic structures and policy requirements of regions, as well as leading to immigration which challenged the indigenous cultures of two of the historic nationalities, the Basque Country and Catalonia. This led in the early twentieth century to limited autonomy being restored to Catalonia.

In the 1930s the Republican Government granted regional autonomy to

EUROPA 1(2/3) 1994 85-97 © Intellect Ltd 1994

Catalonia and, belatedly, to the Basque Country and Galicia, as Civil War gripped the country. This served to further renew the cause of greater autonomy for the three historic nationalities. Under Franco all the vestiges of regionalism were swept away, while there was also a sustained attack on virtually all aspects of regional distinctiveness. However, Francoism failed to eradicate regionalism and nationalism. At the time of Franco's death, not only was there a long history of demands for regional autonomy in Spain, but there were large parts of the population who had actually experienced regional autonomy during their own lifetimes. This, in itself, is not sufficient to explain the extraordinary outpouring of regionalist and nationalist demands in post-Franco Spain. To understand this phenomenon, we need to examine three elements: the strength of cultural and linguistic diversity; the impact of uneven development; and the nature of the opposition to Franco's regime.

Cultural differences form the roots of Spanish nationalism. This is illustrated by the way that the growth of political nationalism in the late nineteenth century was preceded by a cultural revival. In turn, it is clear that language lies at the very heart of cultural differences in the case of the three historic national minorities, the Catalans, the Basques and the Galicians. Terradas (1989, p. 115) emphasises this in the case of the Catalans, arguing that their cultural forms are 'not by themselves different from the cultural forms of other nations, it is their association with language that makes them different'. The Catalans provide only one example and the sheer scale of linguistic diversity in Spain is impressive: an estimated one quarter of the population of Spain do not speak Castillian as their first language.

The most distinctive language is the Basque Country's *Euskera*, which is not an Indo-European language and which does not even have recognisable distant cousins amongst the other European languages. It is a minority language within the Basque Country, being spoken by some 300,000-350,000 persons. Even in its heartland, Gipuzkoa, there are fewer Basque speakers than there are Castillian speakers. The numbers, however, belie the symbolic importance of the language for 'the singularity of *Euskera* encouraged the belief that the Basques were a race apart' (Sullivan, 1988, p. 2), with a right to be independent of both Spain and France. Galician and Catalan are less differentiated from Castillian than is Basque, but both are clearly identified as separate languages, and play crucial roles in nationalist politics. In the case of Galicia, Diaz Lopez (1982, p. 404) writes that 'the language aside from being the most radical and representative element of Galician culture, is what conferred on it the character of a differentiated people with a right to political autonomy'. Language and culture were and are also at the very heart of Catalan nationalism. Their role in the revival of nationalism in the late nineteenth century has already been noted, and it was language which was again the immediate focus for much of the opposition to Francoism. Franco brutally suppressed the use of Catalan in most areas of non-domestic life after the Civil War. Conditions were relaxed in the 1960s and 1970s but mostly at the popular level. Catalan was not recognised as an official language or at the level of high culture, so that at best it faced the prospect of becoming a rustic or folk curiosity. This was to be one of the rallying points amongst Catalan opposition groups in the 1960s (Keating, 1988, p. 213).

The language issue has necessarily been simplified in this discussion. Catalan, for example, is spoken outside of Catalonia - in Valencia and the Balearic Islands - while in parts of the region, such as the Val d'Aran, it is not the dominant language. Castillian is also not a simple unified language for there are important dialects in Andalusia, Asturias and the Canary Islands. In turn, each of these regions is socio-culturally diverse; in the case of Andalusia, for example, this is because the region has 'never had a single, centrifugal city like Barcelona or Bilbao to provide a hegemonic cultural epicentre' (Gilmore, 1981, p. 59). The result of this linguistic and cultural diversity is that Spain is a multipolar society (Guerra, 1989, p. 59), and regionalism and nationalism have flourished around these poles. While the central role of language and culture is unquestionable, these acquired greater potency because of the pressures emanating from uneven economic development. When industrialisation took root in the nineteenth century, it was largely concentrated in three regions: Asturias and especially the Basque Country and Catalonia. The latter two were precisely the regions where the sense of cultural separateness was greatest. In contrast, the political core of the country - Madrid - remained relatively underdeveloped. Quite apart from the perception of Madrid as being a hindrance to the development of the more dynamic regions, there was also potential for conflicts over external policies. This was exemplified by the 1898 Spanish-American War. There was little enthusiasm for this conflict in Catalonia. Yet it was Catalan industry which was to suffer from the resultant loss of protected markets when Spanish colonies in the Carribean and the Pacific secured their independence from the faltering imperial power.

Massively uneven development in the 1950s and the 1960s also contributed to the revival of nationalism and regionalism. During the years of 'the Spanish miracle', growth was again concentrated into the three traditional industrial regions, together with Madrid. Later, there was diffusion of growth to regions such as Valencia, the Balearic Islands and Aragon. However, large parts of Western, Central and Southern Spain remained relatively underdeveloped and figured amongst the poorest regions in Europe. This had three effects. First, it fostered resentment in Catalonia and the Basque Country that they were having to subsidise the poorer regions. Secondly, in the longer term, it meant the existence of a large rump of economically disadvantaged regions which would pose difficult questions of equity and territorial justice in the process of creating regional autonomies in the 1980s. Thirdly, and more immediately, it led to large scale migration from the poorer regions of Spain to the more prosperous ones. In particular, it brought large numbers of Castillian-speakers into the Basque Country and Catalonia. Combined with the Francoist restrictions on the use of non-Castillian languages, this led to real fears that these regions could be culturally overwhelmed. The large proportions of immigrants in these regions posed difficulties for the nationalist movements which tried to represent both the repressed masses as a whole against Francoism and the distinctive cultures of their native peoples. This was to prove particularly difficult for the Basque separatist groups and led to consistent and almost endemic splits in both the military and the political arenas of Basque nationalism (Sullivan, 1988). Nevertheless, it was the cultural challenge which accompanied the arrival of the immigrant populations that was to give a sense of urgency to the nationalist revivals in the 1960s.

The third key element in the revival was that regionalism and nationalism became associated with resistance to the centralism and, indeed, the very existence, of Franco's regime. There had been an earlier precedent for this in the late nineteenth century, when attempts by the Liberals to curb the traditional rights of the regions had driven the Basques and the Catalans to the Carlist cause. After the end of the Civil War, Franco imposed strong central and political control over Spain, coupled with the persecution of non-Castillian languages and culture. When the opposition to Francoism began to re-emerge after the 1940s this was very much centred on Catalonia and the Basque Country where the twin processes of resistance to autocracy and centralism were mutually reinforcing. This would also have longer term implications for the transition to democracy, as Keating (1988, p. 108) has emphasised: 'Franco's persecution certainly crushed the Basque and Catalan movements but, in so doing, created an enhanced sense of anti-regime solidarity in those regions and ensured that any return to democracy would need to have a regional dimension'. This is a theme that we return to in the next section of the paper.

Turning to regionalism in Portugal, there are immediate contrasts evident compared to the Spanish experience. There are no substantial linguistic differences within Portugal, but there has been a pattern of uneven development with economic growth being concentrated in the coastal zone between Setubal and Braga. Most of the remainder of the country remained relatively underdeveloped until comparatively recently. Portugal, similarly to Spain, has also been subject to a prolonged period (1926-74) of centralist dictatorial government in the twentieth century. Yet there have been no regionalist or nationalist movements of any note. It is not that there are no regional differences within Portugal. There are major differences in economic and social structures, between the littoral and the interior, between the North and the South, and between the mainland and the islands (Lewis and Williams, 1981). In this respect, it can be argued that Portugal's Alentejo has more in common with Spain's Andalusia, and the Minho has more in common with Galicia, than either has with each other. The reasons why these socio-economic contrasts have not led to regionalist movements are to be found in the processes of state formation, a shared language and culture, and the role of Lisbon in the life of the country, especially of its élites.

The key point in the history of state formation in Portugal is that the State came into existence before the nation, in the circumstances of military reconquest from the Moors; this greatly facilitated centralisation (Valente, 1983). This meant that, unlike in Spain, the construction of the State was due solely to conquest and not to alliances between states (Feijo, 1989). The boundaries of the State had been established by the first half of the 14th century, and the nation was formed within these. Then in the fifteenth and the sixteenth centuries, there was another period of conquest, when 'the adventure of discoveries and colonial expansion stressed the atlanticisation of the settlement pattern and contributed to the unity of a country turned towards the sea' (Gaspar, 1984, p. 3). Within these boundaries there was formed a nation with a single shared language. Moreover, by 1500, with a few exceptions, Portuguese had evolved to become a clearly separate language from Galician. The importance of this close association of a distinctive language with a single unified country was immense, a point that is underlined by comparisons with Spain.

There are also a number of other reasons for the strong unity of state and nation in Portugal, including the absence of significant ethnic minorities and the existence of a shared religion; these served to diminish although not to eliminate regional cultural differences. The unchallenged primacy of Lisbon in the urban hierarchy, and strong levels of inter-regional migration, also served to strengthen national identity. Of even greater importance - and here again we have a contrast with Spain – was the early emergence of a dominant class, the nobility, which assumed the role of national leadership and solidarity formation. Later this role passed to the urban bourgeoisie. Pina-Cabral (1989, p. 15) writes that 'It is the existence of solidly entrenched urban political and economic élites that explains the apparent unquestioned continuity of Portuguese identity'. The migration of these élites to Lisbon and their education in Coimbra or Lisbon universities further underlined this hegemony.

Virtually the only instance of separatism in modern Portuguese history is to be found in the Azores. Even here there is no sustained history of separatism (Coutinho, 1978), but rather a minor upsurge in the 1970s, related especially to the drift in Portuguese politics to the far left during the course of the unpredictable transition to parliamentary democracy, 1974-1976 (see Gallagher, 1979). There are two grounds on which a regionalist movement could be mobilised; firstly, remoteness from the centres of economic and political power on the mainland, and secondly the prevalence of low incomes which are only one half of the Portuguese average. The fact that these have never provided a basis for more than a rudimentary regionalist movement is predicated on four features of the islands' relationships with the mainland (Lewis and Williams, 1993). First, prior to their colonisation these were uninhabited islands so that their economies and societies have never known a historical evolution independent of the mainland's. Secondly, the education of the island's élites has cemented their links with national élites. Thirdly, the distances between the nine occupied islands in the archipelago, and differences in their economic and social structures, militate against a united Azorean movement. Finally, while there are differences in folk culture between the islands and the mainland, these do not extend to high culture.

While the discussion so far has emphasised the historical bases for the presence or lack of regionalist tendencies in the two countries, much of the character of regionalism and the detailed forms of regional government have been shaped during the two decades since the end of the dictatorships. These are considered in the following sections, commencing with the experience of Spain.

2. La España de las Autonomías: the accommodation of regionalist demands after Francoism

According to Lausen (1986), Spain resembles an inverted centre-periphery model. The principal feature of this model is that the prime instinct of the centre is to retain power rather than to promote economic integration and growth. The result is an unstable territorial system in which there is oscillation between repressive centralism and unstable decentralisation. By the latter years of the Franco regime, repressive centralism, together with the social tensions related to uneven development and the lack of democratic channels for regional representation, had brought about a regional backlash of varying intensity throughout Spain. The most extreme expression of this was to be found in the Basque Country where ETA, after its Fifth Assembly in 1966-67, had launched an escalating campaign of violence against the regime, culminating in the assassination of Prime Minister Carrero Blanco in 1973. Given the political construction of Francoism, the state's only response to this was increased repression and brutality which had the effect of mobilising further support for ETA; this was particularly marked in the state's handling of the Burgos trial in 1970, which led to strong reactions in both the Basque Country and in the world's press (Sullivan, 1988). While the responses in Catalonia and Galicia were far less violent, the depth of regional sentiment was no less, leastways in Catalonia.

The tensions in the regions, and the close association of Francoism with centralism, meant that after 1975 'a solution to the regional problem was considered top priority for the new regime. In the early years of the transition to democracy it was felt that these tensions could endanger the democratic process and even the territorial integrity of Spain' (Guerra, 1989, p. 21). While decentralisation was top of the agenda, there was little agreement as to the form that this should take. A regionalist model which made special provisions for the historic nationalities - the Basques, the Catalans and the Galicians - offered the quickest and simplest solution. But this had two flaws: it would give political privileges to what were already (except for Galicia) economically-favoured regions; and its very exceptionalism would irritate right-wing hardliners in the armed forces and other areas of the state apparatus. The alternative was the broad sweep of federalism offering a similar package of decentralising measures to all regions. This model also had its drawbacks, not least in that there was no agreement in all parts of Spain as to what constituted regions. Therefore, the implementation of any federalist solution was bound to be too fast for some regions and far too slow for others, such as Catalonia and the Basque Country.

In their manifestos for the 1977 election, all the major parties, except the Alianza Popular (which favoured administrative decentralisation), committed themselves to a version of one of these two models. The victorious *Union del Centro Democrático* (UCD) party favoured a flexible formula whereby the constitution guaranteed the right to autonomy but the initiative for autonomy was given to the regions themselves (Newton, 1983, pp. 105-106). This was reflected in the 1978 Constitution which, inevitably, was a compromise between the two models; it advanced a regionalist model in the short term and a federalist model for the longer term (see Bernecker, 1990). It was a concoction that Pi Sunyer (1988, p. 2) has fittingly called *café para todos*.

The 1978 Constitution is based on three main principles: the unity of the state, regional autonomy, and inter-regional solidarity. Formally, Article 2 states that 'the Constitution is based on the indissoluble unity of the Spanish nation, the common and indivisible motherland of all Spaniards, and recognises and guarantees the right to autonomy of the nationalities and regions of which it is composed and the common links that bind them together'. Each region was given the opportunity to organise itself into an autonomous community and to draft its own statute of autonomy which would then be submitted to the parliament for approval. In practice, three main routes were laid down for achieving autonomy:

 a) The regions with a historic claim to autonomy were offered relatively faster routes to relatively higher levels of autonomy. These were defined as the regions which, in the past (that is, in the 1930s, during the Second Republic), had voted for autonomy in a referendum. As such, it included the three historic nationalities: Catalonia, the Basque Country and Galicia.

 b) A provision was made for other regions to argue that they had exceptional cases for higher levels of autonomy. Eventually, four regions - Andalusia, Valencia, Navarre and the Canaries - were able to avail themselves of this route.

 c) The remaining regions were offered lower levels of autonomy during the first five years, but could then seek to revise and increase their autonomous powers subject to a maximum ceiling level. Ten regions were to take this route and all were to revise their autonomy statutes after the first five years.

It was inevitable that any model would generate tensions between Madrid and the regions as to the extent of regional autonomy. However, the very flexibility of the model exacerbated the conflict; the historic regions felt that they were insufficiently privileged and differentiated from the other regions, which in turn considered that they were being discriminated against compared to Catalonia, the Basque Country and Galicia. Given that the Constitution allowed for negotiation of the range and level of powers to be decentralised from Madrid, the end result was an enormous and confusing variety of autonomous statutes. Implementation of the Constitution has been slow and beset with difficulties. Catalonia and the Basque Country were successful in getting their statutes approved relatively quickly in 1979; these provided for significant antonomous powers, including the rights to establish autonomous education systems, separate police forces, and independent (of Madrid) television networks. The Basque and Catalan languages also acquired official status alongside Castillian. These measures were particularly important in meeting the demands of the Catalans for cultural autonomy. Thereafter, the conservative elements within the UCD Government sought to reduce the level of autonomy offered to the other regions, and to delay the process of regionalisation. As a result, Galicia's statute was not finally approved until 1981. Andalusia was next in line and the government now sought to increase the qualifying hurdles for regions seeking autonomy. In the referendum in Andalusia to approve the establishment of an autonomous region, there was an overall majority in favour, but there was a failure to obtain 50% of the votes cast in just one province. Under the new rules for the referenda, this meant that the motion had failed, and the government seemed to have halted the swelling tide of regionalism. However, this proved to be 'a pyrrhic victory' (Newton, 1982, p. 30). There was a strong backlash in the region against the undemocratic procedures for the referenda, and this actually served to mobilise support for the cause of autonomy. Eventually, a second referendum was held on the revised basis of simple majority voting in the region as a whole. The second ballot produced an overwhelming vote in favour of autonomy for Andalusia.

In 1981 there was a dramatic turn of events when there was an attempted coup. Given the UCD Government's, and later the Socialist Governments' fears of being outflanked by the right, this added to the pressures to slow down the reforms. Clark (1987, p. 140) has a more cynical view of events, and believes that the national parties in the late 1970s had courted the support of the regionalist and nationalist parties while they needed their support in the democratisation process, but by the 1980s 'Spain's élites see no need to continue the transfer of power to the Autonomous Communities'. Which of these explanations is more accurate is a matter of debate. However, the outcome was decisive: the UCD Government, with the support of the Socialist opposition, introduced in 1982 the *Ley Orgánica de Armonización del Proceso Autonómico* to harmonise and limit Spain's regionalism programme. It ordained that all other regions were to take the slow route to autonomy and, retrospectively, reduced the powers that had already been granted to the Basque Country and Catalonia. However, this was not the end of the saga; in 1983 the Constitutional Court ruled that large parts of the new law were unconstitutional (Pi-Sunyer, 1988, p. 8). Thereafter, there was rapid approval of all the remaining statutes of autonomy, and regional elections were held in May 1983. As stated previously, ten regions had to take the slow route to autonomy, being granted relatively limited powers until 1989. Thereafter, all the regions had 'full' autonomy although the actual distribution of powers varied from region to region. Despite some limitations in, and some disappointments over, the final territorial settlement, this still represented a major advance for the regions, one that would have seemed unthinkable in the early 1970s.

3. Assessing the Spanish experience

Given the expectations surrounding the programme of regionalism, especially amongst the historic nationalities, and the inauspicious economic climate for any territorial settlement in the 1970s and 1980s (Rhodes and Wright, 1987, p. 15), not to mention the exigencies of the Spanish democratic transition, it was inevitable that the reforms would fail to satisfy all national and regional interest groups. In practice, the process of devolution has often been muddled and indecisive, but by the late 1980s major reforms had been implemented, which were probably unparalleled, in terms of speed and scale, elsewhere in Western Europe. There has been a real decentralisation of power so that even the smallest regions have become responsible for local roads, agriculture, planning economic development and the collection of indirect economic taxes. In the case of the historic nationalities, and some of the other larger regions, they have become responsible for almost all State functions within their boundaries, except the police, the army, foreign policy, major infrastructure and some of the nationalised industries. This has created far greater scope for regional economic policy initiatives. In practice, most regional governments have been relatively conservative in this arena, even if more responsive to regional needs. One of the few radical experiments was the attempt by the Andalusian regional government to introduce land reforms so as to expropriate and redistribute the lands of under-used latifundist estates; this was blocked by the central government and the constitutional court. Instead, most of the regions have directed their attention to education and culture. In Catalonia the reforms have enabled equal status to be given to Catalan alongside Castillian, and Catalan television and radio stations have been established. While this has generated new conflicts with the Castillian-speaking immigrants in these regions, it has also met some of the immediate demands of the historic nationalities.

One of the key tests in any regional autonomy settlement is the rearrangement of financial powers between the centre and the regions. In this respect, the reforms have been decidedly conservative. The Basque Country and Catalonia have been given special rights because of their historic *fueros* and are empowered to collect all taxes within their territories, except customs, petrol and tobacco levies, even though most of the tax rates are dictated by Madrid. However, in the case of the other regions, 98% of their revenue comes from the centre; 57% is in the form of tied grants while 41% comes as block transfers, which offers some degree of autonomy in spending (Hebbert, 1990, p. 126). In contrast, only 2% comes from their own taxes, although many regions supplement this with other local sources of income, including lotteries. Initially, the levels of these financial transfers from the centre were based on bilateral negotiations with the regional authorities. Later they were to be based on formula-funding involving criteria such as population and per capita incomes, so that there would be an in-built redistributive bias.

In addition, two other redistributive mechanisms were created to assist the poorer regions: special grants were made available to regions with sub-standard levels of services; and the Interterritorial Compensation Fund redistributes up to 30% of all new public investment to the least-favoured regions. This fund was actually instituted in 1984 and it determined the levels of 'compensation' on the basis of four indices: per capita income, the migration balance, unemployment and surface area. In 1985, this meant that the largest transfers were made to Andalusia (27%) and to Galicia (10%) (Donaghy and Newton, 1987, p. 106). While there is a strong case for such transfers on the grounds of equity, the transparency of the mechanisms used has made them highly political. As a result, financial devolution has been, and is likely to remain, a major point of contention between the regions and Madrid.

The process of inter-regional transfers is critical for the future of Spain which remains a country with deep regional economic differentials. Despite the dynamism of the Spanish economy in the 1980s, some of the poorest regions in the EC are to be found in Spain in, for example, Extremadura and Andalusia. At the other extreme are Barcelona and Madrid which have claims to be considered world cities. One of the ironies of *La España de las Autonomías* has been the increasing economic dominance of Madrid, which has more than one third of all corporate headquarters and has attracted a disproportionate share of foreign direct investment. As Hebbert (1990, p. 135) notes: 'Whatever the centre has lost in the devolution of administrative and political power, it has regained in the concentration of corporate power'. The claims on central government resources to redress these imbalances are immense, and the very existence of the regional assemblies and governments has created potent channels for the articulation of such regional demands. As a result, in the 1993 parliamentary elections, the People's Party made strong advances in Valencia and other regions by claiming that the Socialist Government had neglected them by concentrating central expenditure on projects such as the high speed Madrid-Seville rail link. Such disputes over discretionary central expenditure serve to reinforce those over formula funding.

Another major problem – and perhaps an inevitable one – has been the enormous differences between the regions in terms of regional identity. While some regions and nationalities have very strongly-developed collective identities, others such as Murcia and La Rioja are considered to be little more than artificial constructions designed to fill in awkward gaps in the map of the regions. There are also major differences in population size, ranging from about 260,000 in La Rioja to about 7 million in Andalusia; this has meant that there are strong differences in the resources available to these regions and in the functions which it is appropriate to devolve to them. Finally, there are also differences between the large multi-province regions such as Castilla-Leon and Andalusia, and the single province ones such as Cantabria. While this has caused difficulties in the short term, especially in the transfer of powers, in the longer term the very existence of these regions will probably lead to the reinforcement of the sense of regional identity in even the weakest of the new regions.

One of the major tests of the new regional system must be the extent to which it has met the demands of regional and national populations and interest groups. The foregoing discussion has made it clear that, thus far, there has been greater progress in respect of culture and education than in economic policy. However, the experience of autonomy to date has fired the desire for further devolution. In particular, the historic nationalities, and some of the other regions, are demanding a more radical redistribution of financial autonomy from the centre to the regions. Despite these reservations, the regional reforms have changed the political landscape of Spain in many significant respects. Nowhere is this clearer than in the Basque Country where the twin processes of democratisation and regionalisation have removed much of the support for violent action by ETA and other groups. While it is true that Herri Batasuna – which has refused to condemn violence – still regularly attracts the support of 14–16% of the electorate (Ross, 1991), this is an exception. Most Basque parties – which together attract one half to two third of electoral support – are in favour of the democratic process, so that violence is no longer seen as a legitimate route to further autonomy and independence.

4. Portugal: Decentralisation in the post-dictatorial era
Portugal during Salazar's dictatorship had been a highly centralised country. The economy had been run on corporatist lines with even minor investment and other decisions having to be referred to Lisbon. Local government financial autonomy had also been virtually eliminated as part of the regime's strategy for controlling public expenditure. It was inevitable therefore that the democratic transition would have to address the issue of decentralisation. However, the lack of regionalist issues and movements in Portugal, compared to Spain, meant that this was given a relatively low priority.

The 1976 Constitution established two main levels of sub-national administration and government: *regioes administrativas* and the municipalities, the *concelhos*. There are direct elections for the municipal councils, while the regional assemblies were to be partly elected directly and partly by the municipal assemblies. Democratic elections for the municipalities were held almost immediately, and they have also been granted a small degree of financial autonomy. However, the establishment of the regional assemblies became bogged down in a long and fruitless debate about territorial boundaries (Porto, 1984), and at present the regionalisation process is best described as being suspended. In contrast, 'The local state was rebuilt and revitalised after 1974 and played an outstanding role in the process of change in Portuguese society and in adaptation to the economic crisis' (Gaspar, 1990, p. 110). The upgrading of social provision and of infrastructure in the towns and villages of Portugal bears powerful testimony to the achievements of the municipalities. There is now a prevalent view that the time for regional reform is past, that given the size and uniformity of Portuguese society there is no need for another tier of government, and that whatever resources are available should be employed to strengthen the municipalities which have a proven track record.

To some extent, the course of Portuguese electoral politics bears testimony to the strength of this argument. In the 1970s and the early 1980s there was a distinctive socio-geographical basis to the electoral support of the main parties (Lewis and Williams, 1984). The Communist Party's support was rooted amongst the urban and rural proletariat of the Alentejo and the greater Lisbon region, while the right-wing Social Democratic and Centre Democratic Parties support was greatest amongst the small-scale farming areas of the north and the centre, and the smaller towns and cities. In contrast, the Socialist Party seemed to be able to draw support from across most regions and social groups. However, by the time of the 1991 election – which saw a second outright win for the Social Democratic Party – the pattern had changed (Corkhill, 1992). Both the

Communist and Centre Democratic Party seemed to be in long-term decline as Portugal moved towards a two-party system, in which the role of regional differences had diminished substantially. At the same time, the most controversial of regionalist issues - land reform - has also passed from the political agenda.

The one exception to this lack of focus on regionalist questions in Portugal is to be found in the Atlantic island, Madeira, and the Azores. Even here, regionalism was important in politics only in the mid-1970s. However, this never amounted to a substantial political movement, and the regionalist parties never attracted any significant level of political support (Gallagher, 1979). The reasons for this have been discussed earlier in this paper (but see also Lewis and Williams, 1993). Over time, there has actually been a diminution of electoral differences between the island and the mainland. In the 1970s, the strong support given to the Social Democratic Party placed the islands well to the right of the mainland political spectrum. Subsequently, the progress made by the PSD in national politics has lead to a convergence in electoral behaviour.

While regionalist movements have never been particularly deep-rooted, or been able to claim much support in the islands, they were given a surprisingly high degree of autonomy in the 1976 Constitution. The reasons for this lie in the particular climate for democratic change in Portugal and in the reaction to the centralism that was associated with Salazarism. Under the Constitution, both the Azores and Madeira were granted directly-elected assemblies and Presidents. The assemblies enacted their own laws, subject to constitutional constraints and the right of veto of the Portuguese parliament. They can also table, or move amendments to, legislation in the national assembly. Additionally, they have considerable financial autonomy in retaining most of the tax revenues collected on the islands. However, they do also have to rely on budgetary supplements from Lisbon and the level of these is one of the few serious points of conflict in relations with the capital.

5. Conclusion: Iberia's regions in the future
Territorial/cultural identities are composed of several diverse elements. In Spain, the late 1970s and the 1980s were occupied with asserting the regional part of these identities. After a prolonged battle with the centre, major gains were secured by the regions and the nationalities by the end of the 1970s. At the same time, the very process of regional self-assertion helped to raise regional consciousness even in those regions where it was previously relatively weak, such as La Rioja and Cantabria. Nevertheless, this is only one of several competing notions of identity. For example, Pina Cabral (1989, p. 5) writes that 'even today, amongst the peasant population of the Alto Minho, the medieval notion of the unity of Christendom still holds great sway'. In the 1980s the most interesting question is the role that a European identity will play in Iberia.

To some extent a European identity has gradually been formed ever since the collapse of Portugal's and Spain's colonial dominance after the seventeenth century. International isolation following the dictatorships and, in Spain's case, the Civil War, limited the process of forming a European identity. However, since the end of dictatorship, and accession to the EC, Eurobarometer polls have consistently shown that within Western Europe, Spanish and Portuguese people have some of the highest levels of attachment to European and EC identities. This is particularly fostered by the Spanish regionalist parties which have seized upon the notion of the 'Europe of the Regions'. In Catalonia and the Basque

Country it has become common to see the regional flag and the European Community flag being flown together, with the Spanish flag conspicuously absent. This has particular appeal for those regional or nationalist parties which wish to emphasise that their outlook is international rather than parochial. This has even offered a useful political platform for the fiercely separatist Herri Batasuna party in the Basque Country, which is implacably opposed to any form of membership of the Spanish state. Needless to say, the debate about the reduced role of the state in the light of the Maastricht agreement, has fuelled the idea of the 'Europe of the Regions' amongst Spain's regionalist and nationalist parties.

These comments are not meant to imply that the Spanish state is doomed to whither away, even in the territories of the historic nationalities. The Spanish state has endured the double transition of democratisation and regionalisation, while most regionalist and nationalist parties have learned to co-exist in coalition governments in many regions. Following, the inconclusive results of the 1993 election, it is likely that similar working relationships will emerge at the national level. The price of the co-operation of the regionalist parties – whether Basque or Catalan – with the Socialist Party is likely to be a further decentralisation of powers, either to the historic nationalities or to all regions. With a few exceptions, there is in fact no evidence that most of the regional populations and parties are seeking any more than this. Regionalism, therefore, seems set to remain an essential element in the political landscape of Spain and, as such, it will mirror the country's incomparably rich cultural diversity. In Portugal, in contrast, it seems highly unlikely that regionalism will be any more potent a political force in the 1990s than it was in the 1980s. Instead, Portugal is likely to remain the model of the unified nation-state in Europe.

References

Bernecker, W. L. (1990), 'Spain and Portugal between regime transition and stabilized democracy', *Iberian Studies*, vol 19, pp. 32-56.

Clark, R. P. (1987), 'The question of regional autonomy in Spain's democratic transition', in R. P. Clark and M. H. Haltzel (eds.), *Spain in the 1980s*, Cambridge, Mass., Ballinger.

Corkhill, D. (1992), 'Imperfect bipolarism? Portugal's political system after the 1991 Parliamentary election', *Journal of the Association for Contemporary Iberian Studies*, vol. 5, pp. 16-23.

Coutinho, A. B. (1978), *Que Futuro para os Acores*, Lisbon, Editorial Caminho.

Donaghy, P. J. and M. T. Newton (1987), *Spain: A Guide To Political and Economic Institutions*, Cambridge, Cambridge University Press.

Feijo, R. C. (1989), 'State, nation and regional diversity in Portugal: an overview', in R. Herr and J. H. R. Polt (eds.), *Iberian Identity: Essays on the Nature of Identity in Portugal and Spain*, Berkeley, Institute of International Studies.

Gallagher, T. (1979), 'Portugal's relations with her Atlantic territories', *The World Today*, March.

Gaspar, J. (1984), 'The unity and individuality of Portugal', *Iberian Studies*, vol. 13, pp. 3-7.

Gaspar, J. (1990), 'The new map of Portugal', in M. Hebbert and J. C. Hansen (eds.), *Unfamiliar Territory: The Reshaping of European Geography*, Aldershot, Avebury Press.

Gilmore, D. D. (1981), 'Andalusian regionalism: anthropological perspectives', *Iberian Studies*, vol. 10, pp. 58-67.

Guerra, L. L. (1989), 'National and regional pluralism in Contemporary Spain', in R. Herr and J. H. R. Polt (eds.) *Iberian Identity: Essays on the Nature of Identity in Portugal and*

Spain, Berkeley, Institute of International Studies.

Hebbert, M. (1990), 'Spain - A Centre-Periphery Transformation', in M. Hebbert and J. C. Hansen (eds.), *Unfamiliar Territory: The Reshaping of European Geography*, Aldershot, Avebury Press.

Keating, M. (1988), *State and Regional Nationalism: Territorial Politics and the European State*, London, Harvester-Wheatsheaf.

Lausen, J. R. (1986), *El Estado Multi-Regional - España Descentráda*, Madrid, Alianza Editorial.

Lewis, J. R. and A. M. Williams (1984), 'Social cleavages and electoral performance: the social basis of Portuguese political parties, 1976-1983', *West European Politics*, vol. 7, pp. 119-37.

Lewis, J. R. and A. M. Williams (1981), 'Regional uneven development on the European periphery: the case of Portugal', *Tijdschrift voor Economische en Sociale Geografie*, vol. 72, pp. 81-98.

Lewis, J. R. and A. M. Williams (1993), 'Regional autonomy and the European Communities: the view from Portugal's Atlantic islands', *Regional Policy and Politics* (forthcoming).

Lopez, C. E. D. (1982), 'The politicization of Galician cleavages', in S. Rokkan and D. W. Urwin (eds.), *The Politics of Territorial Identity: Studies in European Regionalism*, London, Sage.

Newton, M. T. (1982), 'Andalusia: The Long Road to Autonomy', *Journal of Area Studies*, vol. 6, pp. 27-32.

Newton, M. (1983), 'The peoples and regions of Spain', in D. S. Bell (ed.), *Democratic Politics in Spain*, London, Frances Pinter.

Payne, S. (1971), 'Catalan and Basque nationalism', *Journal of Contemporary History*, vol. 6, pp. 15-51.

Pi-Sunyer, O. (1988), 'Catalan politics and Spanish democracy: an overview of a relationship', *Iberian Studies*, vol. 17, pp. 1-16.

Pinha-Cabral, J. de (1989), 'Sociocultural differentiation and regional identity in Portugal', in R. Herr and J. H. R. Polt (eds.), *Iberian Identity: Essays on the Nature of Identity in Portugal and Spain*, Berkeley, Institute of International Studies.

Porto, M. (1984), 'Regional development in Portugal: the institutional framework', *Iberian Studies*, vol. 13, pp. 7-16.

Rhodes, R. A. W. and V. Wright (1987), 'Introduction', *West European Politics*, vol. 10, no. 4 (Special Issue on 'Tensions in the Territorial Politics of Western Europe'), pp. 1-20.

Ross, C. (1991), 'Towards the Basque elections of 1990: the nationalist realignment of 1986-1989 and its effects', *Journal of the Association for Contemporary Iberian Studies*, vol. 4, pp. 49-59.

Sullivan, J. (1988), *ETA and Basque Nationalism: The Fight for Euskadi 1890-1986*, London, Routledge.

Tamames, R. and T. Clegg (1984), 'Spain: regional autonomy and the democratic transition', in M. Hebbert and H. Machin (eds.), *Regionalization in France, Italy and Spain*, London, London School of Economics, International Centre for Economics and Related Disciplines.

Terradas, I. (1989), 'Catalan Identities', in R. Herr and J. H. R. Polt (eds.), *Iberian Identity: Essays on the Nature of Identity in Portugal and Spain*. Berkeley, Institute of International Studies.

Valente, V. P. (1983), *Tentar Perceber*, Lisbon, Imprensa Nacional.

Valle, T. del (1989), 'Basque ethnic identity at a time of rapid change', in R. Herr and J. H. R. Polt (eds.) *Iberian Identity: Essays on the Nature of Identity in Portugal and Spain*, Berkeley, Institute of International Studies.

Regionalism in the United Kingdom
Alan Butt Philip

1. Introduction

Many observers of British society and much of public opinion would deny that regionalism is an issue in the United Kingdom in the 1990s. Such a standpoint reflects a lack of regional consciousness in much of southern Britain and a lack of knowledge of, or even sympathy with, other parts of the British state. Electors often need to be reminded that the UK is comprised of four nations, England, Scotland, Wales and part of Ireland, as well as the Channel Isles and the Isle of Man; or that indigenous languages other than English are spoken in Britain – particularly Welsh (spoken by around 500,000) and Scots Gaelic (spoken by about 80,000). For the purpose of this chapter, the nationalist demands of Scotland, Wales and Northern Ireland will be considered alongside the less obvious regional demands of England itself, even though the arguments for separate recognition of different national identities and demands is of a much larger scale and ideological order than those advanced for regionalism all round. In any case, development within the British constitutional system of stronger political institutions for the different nations of Britain is increasingly seen as contingent upon the acceptance of a set of regional institutions for England. Despite a public rhetoric which denies and denigrates regionalism (at the level of national government and the tabloid press), there are several indications that the regional issue will not disappear and that it is having to be addressed, albeit piecemeal, by central government. As the crisis of legitimacy facing Britain's political institutions and élites deepens, it is likely that the regional issue broadly defined will once more occupy the centre of the political agenda as it did for a time in the 1970s. What was not resolved then may yet have to be resolved in the late 1990s.

2. Origins and History

The origins of the UK's reluctant entanglement with regionalism are various. These range from the nationalist claims of Scotland and Wales which have had to be accommodated by the British political system since the 1880s; the political settlement of the Irish question in 1921 which led to the creation of a largely self-governing province of Northern Ireland; and the practical administrative and occasionally decentralist demands of the English government and political class. The regional dimension in British politics has ebbed and flowed, but it has never died away completely. The spread of political allegiances in the last quarter of the twentieth century suggests that it is likely to be a continuing flashpoint in the British political system, even if occurring episodically.

One of the spin-offs of the paralysis of the United Kingdom regime caused by the campaign for Irish home rule in the nineteenth century was the seriousness with which claims for Scottish and Welsh home rule were taken. The Liberal platform of the late 1890s contained promises of 'home rule all round', a package of devolution measures affecting the whole of the British Isles, even if a precise role for the English regions was not defined. Progress on the Irish question was frustrated by the House of Lords and by the outbreak of the First World War. By 1918 it was clear that a clean break would have to be made between Ireland and the rest of the United Kingdom, an out-turn which choked off the broader British debate on devolution. The nationalist cause in Scotland and in Wales became channelled into political parties dedicated to self-government formed in the 1920s and 1930s. A petition (the Scottish Covenant) demanding a Scottish parliament was signed by two million people in the late 1940s and a similar but much less widely supported petition to parliament was organised in Wales between 1950 and 1955 (see Hanham, 1969 and Butt Philip, 1975). No one at this stage was marching for the cause of English regionalism, nor have they done so since.

The current cycle of devolutionist pressures in the United Kingdom can be traced back to the mid-1960s when a combination of regional economic decline, disillusion with the Labour party and anxiety (in Wales) about cultural change fed a strong political revival of Scottish and Welsh nationalism. The House of Commons was forced to spend much of its time between 1974 and 1979 on devolution legislation which however came to nought as a result of two referenda held in Scotland and Wales in March 1979. Matters in the province of Northern Ireland were also on the move, but in an unrelated way. The inability of the Protestant dominated Unionist Government in the province to deal adequately with the substance of grievances from the minority Catholic population caused the Conservative Government at Westminster under Edward Heath to abolish the provincial government at Stormont in 1972 in favour of direct rule from London. Over twenty years later this remains the position, despite many abortive attempts to re-establish an elected Northern Irish Government based on power-sharing or with entrenched minority rights.

The agitation for greater recognition of Scottish and Welsh devolution has had other political consequences, such as the transfer of new powers and resources to the Scottish Office and the newly-established Welsh Office (1964), the passage of the Welsh Language Act (1967) giving equal validity to Welsh in public administration in Wales, the mobilisation of MPs more frequently into regional groupings to lobby their own party leaderships, and the setting up of a Royal Commission on the Constitution under Lord Kilbrandon, which reported in 1973. Regional policy also attracted greater attention in the 1960s and 1970s before being cut back by Conservative administrations after May 1979. Local government and administration has been a continuing object of attention by successive Tory prime ministers. The formation of the Greater London Council and the six metropolitan county councils in England in 1963 was followed by a wholesale reform of local government in England, Scotland and Wales in 1973-74, abolition of the GLC and the metropolitan counties in the mid-1980s, progressive privatisation of service provision previously undertaken by local councils, and further reviews of local government structure in 1992-94 in order to establish unitary local authorities as widely as possible. Such turmoil is symptomatic of an early phase of institutional reforming zeal, reflecting confidence in the ability of structural changes to improve quality of service, which gave way in the 1980s to a zeal to cut down bureaucracy and to contain burgeoning local government spending. Regional strategic needs and the desirability of creating or building upon existing regional identities have been very low on central government's list of political priorities. Yet the regional dimension has been hard to extinguish, even in England, and shows signs of revival as the millennium approaches, despite the increased centralisation of power in Whitehall and Westminster and the impact of improved physical and media communications upon the attitudes, place of residence and lifestyle of the citizens of Britain.

3. The Devolution Debate

In 1951 the Conservative and Labour parties captured between themselves almost 97 per cent of the total votes cast at the October general election that year. By February 1974 a quarter of the votes cast at the UK general election were cast for parties other than the two largest parties, most of them committed to some form of regional devolution or even more radical reorganisation of the British state. That position has remained broadly unchanged at all subsequent general elections. The vagaries of the British electoral system have meant that these votes have often not been able to be reflected in the distribution of seats in the House of Commons. Yet between 1974 and 1979 the votes of Liberal, Nationalist and Ulster MPs played critical roles in ensuring the survival of Labour Governments in two successive parliaments, and there have been signs since the general election of 1992 that the 'minority parties' are once again becoming critical determinants in the passage through the Commons of significant parts of the Conservative government's programme. With such influence comes the power to re-set the political agenda to include issues related to devolution and regional policy (see Rose, 1982 and Bogdanor, 1979).

The long drawn out attempt to establish assemblies in Scotland and Wales in the 1970s dominated the legislative timetable of the House of Commons and proved extremely divisive for Labour, whose northern English MPs were extremely suspicious of the advantages that would accrue to Scotland and Wales once devolution was in place. The proposals for a scheme of legislative devolution for Scotland and administrative devolution for Wales were eventually submitted to national referendums in each country. The Welsh scheme was roundly rejected by voters by a margin of almost four to one, while the Scottish scheme was approved by a small majority but failed to attract the support of forty per cent of the electorate as required by the Westminster parliament. The whole exercise proved extremely debilitating for the political class as a whole, for no tangible result other than the ultimate demise of the Callaghan government. Yet the arguments had revealed some serious difficulties in trying to set up a scheme of devolution which omitted any consideration of the English dimension. Scottish and Welsh MPs at Westminster would have been able to vote on issues only of concern to England, because devolved assemblies in Scotland and Wales would be responsible exclusively for several policy fields. Northern and south western MPs were alarmed at the autonomy offered to Scotland and Wales but denied to their regions. The Welsh electorate proved very suspicious of anything seen as a sop to Welsh nationalism, and would have been much reassured if the devolution scheme had been part of a package in which the English regions were included.

The incoming Thatcher administration in 1979 was not only ideologically opposed to devolution but had compelling practical reasons for abandoning the whole project. The price of so doing was a progressive alienation of Scottish public opinion during the 1980s. Labour meanwhile was left to sort out its internal differences. No mention of a Welsh assembly, let alone a scheme of regional government for England, was made in its 1983 election manifesto, but by 1987 pledges of action on both had returned. The experience of the 1970s persuaded the Liberals that a federal solution was the only way to avoid the many anomalies that would be introduced by a scheme of piecemeal devolution. Unfortunately, some of their allies in the newly formed SDP, such as Dr David Owen, were contemptuous of federalism - at British or European levels - and the Alliance leadership had to be content to reaffirm the primacy of establishing Scottish and Welsh parliaments as part of a phased introduction of an overall devolutionist structure.

The threat of rising Scottish and Welsh nationalism appeared to have been contained by the Conservatives for much of the 1980s, with SNP representation at Westminster reduced from a high point of 11 MPs in 1974-79 to 3 MPs at the 1987 general election. Scotland continued to be the most promising lever on the British constitution upon which the hopes of all those who argued for home rule, regional devolution and a wider agenda of constitutional reform rested. In the UK as a whole, the cross-party Charter 88 movement was set up in 1988 to argue for a whole set of inter-locking constitutional reforms, including greater regional autonomy, and attracted 40,000 subscribers and some centre-left quality newspaper support. In Scotland itself a broad-based coalition of forces, including the Labour and Liberal Democrat parties, the Church of Scotland and business leaders established a Scottish Convention which met to work out an agreed scheme for a new Scottish parliament. Despite the weakness of the Conservatives north of the border (with 9 MPs at Westminster out of 72), the government of John Major, who succeeded Mrs Thatcher as Prime Minister in November 1990, was able successfully to tar all the non-Conservative supporters with an anti-unionist brush at the April 1992 general election. Against all expectations the Conservative vote increased slightly to twenty-six per cent of those voting in Scotland; 10 Tory MPs were returned to Westminster and the status quo was defended and maintained. Further progress on devolution in Great Britain appears to rest upon the Conservatives losing their majority in the House of Commons, and this essentially will require a change of heart in England.

4. Regional Policy and Administrative Regionalism

Regional policy, defined as the attempt by governments to influence by policy measures the course of economic development in the regions, has a pedigree in the United Kingdom that goes back sixty years. In Britain the principal objective of regional policy has been to maintain or to create employment, whereas in other EC states other objectives have formed part of regional policy, such as land-use and infrastructure planning. Macro-economic policy considerations arising from the danger of overheating the most successful regional economies causing cost-push inflation across the whole national economy have also justified government attempts to rebalance economic growth patterns as between regions all over Western Europe.

The first attempts at UK regional policy were made in the Special Areas Acts of 1934 to 1937 in response to the collapse of employment in the slump years in regions such as South Wales, parts of Durham, Tyneside, West Cumberland and Scotland. This piecemeal approach was developed into a more generalised regional policy following an influential wartime review, the Barlow report. A more or less integrated regional, industrial and employment policy was maintained from the 1940s until the end of the 1970s and the arrival of Mrs Thatcher as Prime Minister (see Smith, 1989).

The methods adopted by central government policy-makers have been used continuously but are often varied in terms of policy mix. The most favoured method has been the provision of capital grants to industry, in the private sector as well as in the public sector, linked to regional development and the creation of jobs. This approach has run into several difficulties. It has usually been addressed to manufacturing industry, when the main sources of job creation were in the service sector. It is increasingly constrained by EC rules (see below), and its efficacy has been strongly challenged by neo-liberal economists. However a major study for the Department of Trade and Industry in 1986 found that much of UK regional policy had been successful in creating nearly 600,000 long term jobs (Moores, Rhodes and Tyler, 1986).

Another instrument that has been used to boost regional development and employment has been the provision of large public funds for public infrastructure in the regions - for motorways and roads, rail electrification, telecommunications, power generation and water supply developments, new towns and, to some extent, new universities. Central government departments have been dispersed in whole or in part to regional locations away from London: the Crown Agents were sent to East Kilbride (near Glasgow), the main social security activity (now the Benefits Agency) went to Newcastle, the Department of Health to Leeds, and the Manpower Services Commission (now part of the Employment and Training Agency) to Sheffield. Economic development institutions have been set up such as the English Estates corporation (now privatised) which built and managed industrial estates, new town and later urban development corporations, regional development agencies in Scotland, Wales and Northern Ireland, and the short-lived National Enterprise Board (1974-1979) (see Butt Philip, 1978). Government grants to subsidise current employment costs in regional undertakings played a major part (notably the Regional Employment Premium and the Temporary Employment Subsidy schemes) in the policy of the 1970s, and these do continue in the 1990s in the public transport field with annual subsidies to the regional operational costs of British Rail and Caledonian MacBrayne's ferry services to the Scottish islands.

The ideological thrust of Mrs Thatcher's governments in the 1980s was clearly in conflict with such interventionist subsidies. Market forces could have been allowed free rein and regional dispersal of firms and employment achieved in the long term as companies moved away from high cost, scarce labour regions to lower cost, rich in labour regions. There were bound to be short term costs in terms of socio-political damage, leapfrogging wage and housing price spirals, and inadequate infrastructures in the expanding areas. Fortunately the theory was never fully tested as the rigidities in the labour and housing markets soon became clear; the famous 'get on your bike' advice given to the unemployed by one senior Tory Government minister, Norman Tebbit, fell foul of the realities of the absence of affordable and available housing in those areas where employment opportunities were greatest. The Thatcher governments therefore never completely abandoned regional policy. They proved fearful of applying their economic philosophy fully in this area, and they were trapped by continuing EC funds for regional development being tied to co-finance by UK central or local government. After major reviews of regional policy in 1983 and 1988, the 'social' justification for regional policy was accepted, but the budget for regional grants continued to be cut in real terms, and the areas eligible to receive such grants greatly reduced in size. Assisted area status was still much sought after in the

1990s, as the key to unlock funds from Brussels, if nothing else, and by 1993 the UK government was adding areas like Portsmouth, Thanet and the East End of London to its list having previously removed areas such as mid-Wales, North Devon and North East Scotland (see Tighe, 1993 and Wintour, 1993).

Conservative Governments may have downgraded regional policy as such since 1979 but they have accepted the case for limited public sector intervention in special areas, where possible linked with private sector finance. This has led to the formation of new designations such as tax-relieved 'enterprise zones', and new appointed bodies directly funded by central government, such as the London Docklands Development Corporation and a host of urban development corporations, operating for example in Bristol, the Black Country and Merseyside inner city areas have had to compete for central government funds in the thirty 'City Challenge' schemes. In 1993 some unification of these separate urban initiatives was announced in the form of new 'City Pride' teams linking local businessmen with civil servants to oversee urban policy implementation (Willman and Burt, 1993). This represents another sign that regional policy is being overtaken by urban policy, and specifically inner city concerns. The bare economic indicators, especially the figures on regional unemployment rates (see Table 1), help to explain why this is so. In parallel with the onset of the 1989-93 recession there has been clear evidence of convergence in the economic circumstances of the various UK regions, although a similar trend predates this. In the twenty-two years since 1971 all regions have seen a rise in unemployment, but whereas the most affected region (Northern Ireland) saw its unemployment rate double from 7 to 14 per cent, the least affected region (the South East) saw its unemployment rate rise almost fivefold from 2 to 10 per cent. The regional differential has thus narrowed over two decades, and this is also true for the movement of regional GDP, although the greatest change has occurred as a result of the most recent recession, whose long term impact cannot yet be assessed.

To an important extent, the condition of regional economic policy remains stronger in Scotland, Wales and Northern Ireland, where specific initiatives have been made and separate political institutions exist to support and to implement them. One reading of the economic convergence noted above is that the separate regional policies of those named areas have indeed proved their worth. In 1966 as a result of regional economic and political pressure a new Highlands and Islands Development Board was set up to stimulate employment and economic development. This was followed in 1975 by the new Scottish, Welsh and Northern Ireland Development Agencies. They offered an integrated, interventionist, hands-on approach to the resolution of long standing regional economic difficulties and appear to have had much success. (The situation in Northern Ireland has proved more difficult than in Scotland and Wales, possibly as a result of the continuing communal conflict there, although the Local Economic Development Unit (LEDU) which assists small firms in Northern Ireland has been very successful). Early Conservative attempts to abolish them in 1979-80 foundered on intense local opposition, including from their own supporters. In the 1990s, the Scottish agencies have been broken up into smaller area-based units and they have been given employment training as well as economic development roles. They may however have lost much of their value as developers and implementers of regional industrial strategies, just because of their smaller scale and local focus.

Undoubtedly a major element in the success of these development agencies has been their close sponsorship and relations with the so-called 'regional' departments of central government - the Scottish Office, the Welsh Office and the Northern Ireland Office, the latter set up shortly after direct rule was re-imposed in 1972. This administrative arrangement has transferred most of the domestic responsibilities of central government in these named areas to the relevant 'regional' department (e.g. agriculture, health, transport, education, environment and employment). The 'regional' departments have enjoyed considerable autonomy, as well as the responsibility for distributing their sizeable block grants for public expenditure which Whitehall has handed down. This has enabled significant differences in the evolution of education policy or the levels of the local 'poll' tax to be funded and sustained. In addition, the much smaller political élites present in these 'regional' capitals have been able to work across departmental boundaries at all levels with considerable ease, away from the gaze of Westminster, shielded from much public accountability, and motivated to work for the common good of their sub-national territory.

This configuration of administrative devolution and regional development agencies working successfully in Scotland, Wales and Northern Ireland has naturally attracted the envious eyes of some English regions. In the 1970s, some of the bigger, quasi-regional authorities set up their own regional enterprise boards with funds from their own employees pension funds, county council grants and some private finance. The West Midlands and Greater London Enterprise Boards even managed to survive - but in much truncated form - the demise of their founding local authorities. Lancashire Enterprises Limited had acquired a national reputation for innovative and enlightened investment and help for local firms. But the aversion to regional approaches in England has been mirrored at this level too with individual local authorities each embarking on their own local economic initiatives, with rare examples of co-operation (such as between Devon and Cornwall, or Yorkshire and Humberside) serving as exceptions that prove the general rule. Some English county councils have argued that they are sufficiently large to count as regions in their own right: Essex (population 1.25 million) is one such council to have pursued this line, even to the point of twinning with the French region of Picardy and setting up a joint representative office in Brussels. At least eight British regions, counties or districts have separate representatives in Brussels, alongside Scotland, Wales and Northern Ireland (see Audit Commission, 1991).

By the end of 1993, two further developments in the organisation of local administration point in contrary directions as regards the future of the regional dimension. On the one hand local government reform is proceeding apace with the Local Government Commission under Sir John Banham being directed to establish unitary local authorities in England, leading to the demise of most county councils. In Scotland the proposed reform of local government announced by Ian Laing, the Secretary of State for Scotland, in the summer of 1993 would abolish all regional councils. The Banham Commission, in sounding out public opinion, is not even asking respondents if they have any sense of regional identity, unlike the Kilbrandon and Redcliffe-Maud commissions of the 1970s (Royal Commission on Local Government in England, 1969 and Royal Commission on the Constitution, 1973). Yet in an attempt by central government to streamline the organisation of central government departments at regional level, Whitehall has proposed to establish new regional directors at a senior level to co-ordinate the work in the standard regions of several government departments (regional economic development, environment, employment and training, industry and transport) and to offer a 'one-stop' shop to firms and local authorities (see White, 1993a and Willman and Burt, 1993). This may indeed be a classic example of top-down regionalism, of devolution rather than decentralisation, but it is almost as if the very fragmentation of local government at base level is driving the Conservative Government inexorably towards the recognition of the region for strategic planning and development purposes, in defiance of its own rhetoric. This may however be at the expense of elected and directly accountable local government (see Capon, 1993).

5. The EC Dimension

Regional policy has become a major concern of the European Community since the late 1960s when EC leaders from the original six member states realised that a strong Community regional policy was an essential accompaniment to the project for economic and monetary union. This interest in regional policy, which was of most concern to Italy, was then exploited strongly in the enlargement negotiations of 1970-71 when the United Kingdom and Ireland, as applicants to join the EC, sought and obtained compensation for their peripheral position relative to the main Community markets. Britain was also keen to establish a budget line, in the form of the new European Regional Development Fund (ERDF), from which it could draw large amounts (initially 28 per cent of the entire Fund) in order to balance some of its potentially large 'net contribution' to the overall EC budget. By the mid 1980s the ERDF had expanded considerably on the back of further additions to the membership of the Community and was increasingly being organised in combination with the European Social Fund (ESF) and the guidance section of the fund financing the whole of the common agriculture policy. The three funds, the so-called structural funds, will account for around one third of EC budgetary spending by the year 2,000, compared with less than ten per cent of spending in 1980.

A more long-standing constraint on the development of national regional policies has been the Community's control over state aids, using Articles 92 to 94 of the EEC Treaty. The logic of EC competition policy demands that national governments should not be permitted to distort competition and subsidise 'lame duck' enterprises which are otherwise uncompetitive and not viable. The European Commission (DGIV) in Brussels must therefore authorise any regional development scheme, using state subsidies, in any member state – also any subsidy to a particular sector of industry or to a particular firm. The Commission has tried to make a judgement on the 'objective need' of particular regions using its own consistently comparable data of regional deprivation and divergence, and establishing a sliding scale of permitted levels of subsidy (in terms of percentage of the whole capital cost of a project) applicable to each region of the Community. While the controls on state aids from Brussels were honoured as much in the breach as in the observance in the 1970s, the drive to complete the single European market begun in 1985 has encouraged successive competition commissioners to apply the rules very comprehensively and to require much more information about, and control over, regional and sub-regional incentive schemes to encourage existing and newly-formed businesses to grow. Although the Commission is permitted to allow subsidies where conditions justify them, this detailed control has nevertheless begun to bite, and contributes significantly to the way UK government departments, local authorities and enterprise agencies can structure their economic incentive packages for regions and areas in difficulty.

In the United Kingdom the process of European integration has thus heightened the role of the Community in the management of regional development at the level of Whitehall, and below. Securing eligibility for receipt of structural funds from Brussels, and then competing for those funds once eligibility is established, has proved to be a major strategic consideration for regions as varied in their needs as the West Midlands, Strathclyde and Devon and Cornwall. As state aids have become more heavily controlled, and fewer job creating investment opportunities presented themselves, so the bulk of EC funding has been more and more devoted to the co-finance of infrastructure projects. Major Whitehall constraints on local authority capital spending have made it increasingly difficult for EC-funded regional schemes to be launched, and there are long-standing disputes between Brussels, Whitehall and local agencies over the extent to which central government pockets money received from the Community rather than passing it down the line: this is the issue of 'additionality', over which the Commission and other member states have made periodic threats to withhold funds from Britain.

These sums received from the structural funds are not inconsiderable – around £900 million per annum, in the late 1980s, nearer £700 million each year in the 1990s. They have acquired extra significance for the regions as UK government spending on regional development grants was cut back sharply in the 1980s. The result has been that regional spending priorities have been increasingly dominated by EC, not UK, eligibility criteria and policy objectives, with the Department of Trade and Industry, the lead department in Whitehall, content to travel along the path toward greater Europeanisation of regional policy (Department of Trade and Industry, 1988). Local and regional authorities' bids for assisted area status, a *sine qua non* for receiving ERDF support, have increasingly had to be made to Brussels as well as to London. Whereas in the mid-1980s only Northern Ireland was deemed by the EC to be worthy of top priority funding from the structural funds, with mid-Wales and Devon and Cornwall obtaining some rural development help, by 1993 Merseyside and the Highlands and Islands were added to the list of 'objective one' regions, and towns in south east England, such as Portsmouth and Margate, were bidding to be included.

EC funding for poorer regions, concentrating mainly upon capital projects for infrastructure and industrial development and vocational training schemes, demands much new activity for UK central and local government, especially as England was stripped of almost all regional administration by the Thatcher administration. Regional development plans have had to be submitted to Brussels on the basis of which Community Support Frameworks, directing EC aid, have been negotiated. Funding from Brussels for integrated operations covering areas in and around Belfast, Birmingham and Glasgow has been conditional upon a regional team of administrators and local representatives being formed to implement and monitor the approved major funding programmes. Regional GDP statistics have, very controversially, had to be prepared in addition to regional unemployment statistics, so that Brussels can take a pan-European view of Britain's regional needs. In the absence of any defined regions in England (other than the over-large eight 'standard' regions), county councils have had to bid for regional status in the eyes of Brussels, or make alliances with their neighbours to do so. Local authorities have had to become increasingly wise to the policies and politics of the European Community, in order to benefit from the myriad programmes, with subsidies attached, emanating from Brussels and in order to comply with and implement, as agents of central government, the letter and the spirit of the Single European Market. They have been instrumental in alerting the Commission to the specific problems of regions facing industrial shutdowns in coal, shipbuilding, steel, defence and other sectors, prompting in turn EC-led targetted conversion programmes like RECHAR, RENAVAL, RESIDER and KONVER respectively. The Commission has seemed to many in local and regional government, for a long time, to be more sympathetic and more in tune with regional needs than Whitehall.

It is not just that the whole administrative structure of England is unsuited to the structure for developing and administering EC structural fund programmes (the position in Scotland, Wales and Northern Ireland being wholly different) which the Community has laid down for all member states. England lacks a regional tier of administration, and the small regional outposts of central government departments have not been in the habit of co-operating one with another. The Wilsonian structure of regional economic planning boards and councils from the 1960s was finally dismantled in the early 1980s. Strategic urban planning authorities, such as the Greater London Council and the metropolitan county councils were all broken up in the mid-1980s and not replaced. This left no apparatus in England with which to handle the ever-growing need of Brussels for regional interlocutors and regional economic analysis, as was pointed out by a House of Lords Select Committee in 1984 (House of Lords Select Committee on the European Communities, 1983-84 and 1987-88). By the autumn of 1993, the UK government was forced publicly to announce a reversal of policy and a strengthening of the regional offices of central government departments such as the environment and employment ministries (see White, 1993b). The purpose of these reforms being ostensibly to exercise greater control over the urban development corporations and to enable civil servants to respond better to European initiatives.

Another event in 1993 tellingly illustrated how the process of centralisation of power in the British state is colliding with the development of the European Community. The Maastricht Treaty on European Union provides for the creation of an EC-wide Committee of the Regions to advise the EC institutions on regional needs and issues. The UK government did not oppose the creation of this new quango, having other more important fish to fry in the treaty negotiations, but it proved surprisingly resistant to demands from the House of Commons that all twenty-four UK representatives should be drawn from elected local government councillors. It appears that the Conservative Government would have liked to put British ministers with regional portfolios on their Committee, but MPs - perhaps fighting other battles - decided to insist on a councillors only clause, and the government was defeated.

6. The Region in British Society

Although British society is relatively homogeneous in relation to other European states there are still many factors in its composition which make for diversity, much of which is manifested in differences in the geographical distribution of characteristics, lifestyles and traditions. These differences form much of the basis of regional sentiment and identity in the United Kingdom, as well as the fact of geography itself.

The British population itself has diverse origins. While very few can identify their Norman ancestry, let alone their origins as incoming Jutes and Angles from continental Europe, there is still a keen sense of the different ethnic identities in the Celts in Ireland, the Picts and Scots in Scotland, the Norse people in Orkney and Shetland, and the mixed Celtic-Briton population of Wales. More recent migrations of Irish, Afro-Caribbean and people from the Indian sub-continent have not taken on a regional form but particular urban concentrations. This means that some ethnic differences in Britain have a regional cultural resonance while others do not. This is seen in terms of differences of first language, for example, where the large Urdu, Hindi and Gujurati speaking populations are spread across several urban centres in England, while the smaller population of Welsh speakers (*circa* 500,000) is concentrated in Wales, with especially high concentrations in the north and west of the country. Minority languages specific to the British Isles also occur in Ireland and northern Scotland, being Gaelic in kind. Dialects and the incidence of particular idioms and word forms also have a strong regional distribution throughout Britain as elsewhere.

Popular culture is also subject to regional variations, despite the pervasive influence of nationally organised mass media. Television has important regional opt-outs (especially for Scotland, Wales and Northern Ireland) as regards the BBC, and independent television, apart from its national news service, is completely regional in its organisation. The daily press is even more biased towards London production and orientation, but does have a hard time in selling papers in Scotland and Northern Ireland, where indigenous dailies such as The Scotsman or Belfast Newsletter or regional variations of the national dailies are more favoured. A long campaign led to the creation of a separate largely Welsh medium television channel in 1980 subsidised by the whole independent television network. The arts in general have developed an increasing regional profile, with national orchestras, theatre and dance companies making regular touring appearances in regional centres, and the regional centres themselves developing a substantial artistic life. Part of the Tate Gallery's collection in London has been moved to a new permanent site in Liverpool, while Glasgow has made great strides to develop a cultural profile that rivals that of Edinburgh. Leeds now hosts an internationally recognised piano festival and Birmingham has a symphony orchestra of international standard. Market researchers have found important differences of taste occurring between regions whether it be fashion or food and drink. The Welsh have a penchant for tinned salmon and the Geordies for brown ale, it seems. In sport, the more thriving activities often have regional organisations to implement national rules, as a practical response to supervising events and behaviour of athletes rather than a real expression of regional identity (the Welsh Rugby Football Union excepted!). Some sports do have a particular regional presence, rugby league in northern England, hurling in Ireland, and Highland games in northern Scotland. The voluntary sector also spawns regional organisations as a necessary interface between national and local activities, the more extensive its area of work and activities become. A few trade unions are region-specific such as the Educational Institute of Scotland and the Farmers Union of Wales, while in Ireland trade unions often ignore the border for organisational purposes.

In the world of education there are pronounced differences between Scotland, Wales and Northern Ireland, and the rest of Britain. Thus the break between

Scottish secondary and higher education occurs one year earlier than in England and Wales, and a different examination system and degree course structure results. In Northern Ireland almost all schools are still divided on communal lines, while in Wales, the Welsh language has a special place in the national curriculum and numerous Welsh medium primary and secondary schools and pre-school groups have been set up since the 1950s. The University of Wales has a special federal structure, but this appears to be breaking down (rather as is that of the University of London).

Variations in religious affiliations and observance are also to be found in the regions within the indigenous Christian tradition. Thus church-going in Northern Ireland is a majority pursuit, compared to one in seven of the UK population as a whole. Important Catholic concentrations occur in the West of Scotland, Merseyside and other areas of high Irish immigration since the 1840s. Non-conformist Protestants are strongly concentrated in the South West and North of England, Wales and Northern Ireland. In Scotland a more advanced form of Protestantism prevails, and the Church of Scotland has more than once provided the focus for national campaigns on behalf of the whole nation. The Anglican tradition provides the established state church only in England.

Regional religious differences form part of the reason for regional political variations in voter allegiance. Catholics provide disproportionate support for Labour in central Scotland, and the non-conformist past accounts for a large part of the survival of the Liberal tradition in the west of England. In recent years general elections have demonstrated more pronounced variations by region in the swings of voter support for political parties. The 1987 election saw an ever sharper loss of support for the Conservatives the greater the distance from London, but a favourable swing to the government in the South-East of England (see Butler and Kavanagh, 1988, p. 284). In 1992 the reverse occurred, with the largest swings against the government occurring in the South-East and the South-West (see Butler and Kavanagh, 1992, pp. 324–332). The political battle is somewhat different in both Wales and Scotland where nationalist parties make the party contest a four-way split. In Northern Ireland, none of the British political parties is a significant player in the politics of the province, and the seventeen MPs attending Westminster are drawn from four distinct Northern Irish parties. Political differences of this kind have led the UK parliament to continue to legislate separately for Scotland, with its own Romano-Dutch legal system. Northern Ireland, and occasionally Wales too, also benefits from separate legislation and different standards, where moral and social issues are at stake.

The distribution of public expenditure is also skewed in favour of the more peripheral regions of the UK. In part this reflects the great role the public sector has played in the economic life of such regions (although this is fast diminishing), and in part it reflects different degrees of economic activity among regional populations. The tax take is much greater in southern England where incomes and employment rates are higher. By the same token cuts in welfare payments affect disproportionately those living in areas furthest from London (see Hencke, 1993). The imposition of value added tax on fuel consumption from 1994 will, for reasons to do with the colder climate, bear hardest on those living in the north of Britain. The new uniform business rate introduced in 1990 was intended in part to tax businesses in southern England more heavily than those in the north.

As noted earlier, patterns of employment are regionally distinct, and this affects not only the balance between the private and the public sector, but also the growth and popularity of self-employment. Between 1979 and 1987, for example, self-employment in Great Britain grew by some 52 per cent, but the regional growth varied from Wales (+19%) and Scotland (+21%) to South West England's (+90%) (Department of Employment, 1988). In some respects the regional organisation of major public sector employers such as British Coal and British Steel has atrophied as the industries themselves have declined. The regional organisation of the gas supply industry was abolished in the early 1980s, and is being much reduced in significance at British Rail. Regional organisation has however been institutionalised upon the privatisation of the electricity and water supply industries. Regional health authorities overseeing health care provision will survive only until 1996, but some regionalisation of police functions has occurred and more is being canvassed (*The Guardian*, 22 October 1993 and *The Independent*, 22 October 1993). A major problem with such regional institutions is that the territorial divisions within which they operate almost never coincide across different functions. Where regional provision of public services, of public infrastructure and some strategic planning is called for the ensuing arrangements have been invariably *ad hoc* in nature (e.g. road building) or nothing has been attempted (e.g. waste disposal strategy).

Economic differences between the UK regions have also led to striking divergences in the behaviour of the housing market between the regions in the 1980s and 1990s, the boom of the former especially in the south and east being followed by a major bust. Because home ownership using mortgage finance affects half the population, major differences in purchasing power have emerged between the regions as regards non-housing related expenditure. This in turn has altered the severity and impact of the recession across the regions of the United Kingdom and has contributed to the apparent convergence of regional economic indicators noted above.

The portrait of the UK regions thus depicted is confusing, as regional variations in social, economic, political and cultural life are revealed to have many different, almost kaleidoscopic, configurations. Yet the particular distinctiveness of Scotland, Wales and Northern Ireland emerge clearly and this has been recognised in the arrangement of public administration, and to a lesser extent the law, of these countries. The position in England is less clear-cut, for while regional differences do exist they are by no means so sharply drawn compared with the rest of the United Kingdom, nor do their contours very often overlap. There is no regional administration or government or public life to give shape or form to such regional differences as do exist, or to build up a regional constituency of shared interests. Indeed in many parts of middle and southern England no clear regional identity exists among the population at large. Where some regionalisation of government was beginning to emerge, and an identification with it by public opinion, the institutions were destroyed in 1986, in the case of Greater London much against the views of the electorate. A contributory factor, in addition, has been the much stronger local identities, typically to be found in counties such as Somerset, Cornwall or Durham, which reflect administrative (and socio-cultural) divisions which go back one thousand years. The French *départements* (two hundred years old) and the German *Länder* (less than fifty years old) cannot compete. Changes in communications are making for a reconfiguration of identities and interests. Nationally dominated television, radio and newspapers have spread national perspectives and values to the whole population of Britain, and have contributed to the further marginalisation of regionally based ethnic cultures, provoking a spirited political response. One of the most dramatic of such responses was the hunger strike started by Mr Gwynfor Evans, former Plaid Cymru leader and MP, in 1980 to persuade the new Conservative government to honour its election commitment to establish a separate Welsh fourth television channel. The government succumbed to pressure on this issue.

The shrinking of the separation of the periphery from the core of the UK and its capital as a result of high-speed rail and air travel, and the development of an extensive motorway network, has opened up many previously remote parts of Britain to outside influences and has made the notion of regional government and regional identification more feasible. The great paradox is that just as these possibilities are being opened up, the official position of the UK government could scarcely be more hostile. Indeed one construction to be put upon the administrative and structural reorganisation of government and the public sector pursued since 1979 is that the Conservatives have consciously sought to undermine all large centres of power located away from Westminster with a view to reinforcing the power of central government. A parallel rhetoric can be deployed to claim that the break-up of big local authorities and the waves of privatisation will deliver more local control to consumers, customers and communities. But their margin of control has been reduced by Whitehall strings attached, and by reductions of real capital and real current spending limits. In relative terms central government has won back power from the regions and has ensured that no regional institutions in England with any political weight have survived to challenge Whitehall's priorities. The final irony appears to be that in response to a mixture of excessive fragmentation of local government and EC pressures central government is itself having to re-invent the regional tier of administration, albeit completely under Whitehall control.

7. Conclusion: Why is Britain the odd one out in Europe?

Regionalism was always likely to have difficulty winning political acceptance in the United Kingdom. It appeals to planners and to the politically marginalised, especially those on Britain's periphery, but the idea of regionalism does not sit well within the political culture of the twentieth century British state. Since the Norman conquest in the late eleventh century the ideology of firm central government control over the regions as an essential condition for the survival of the state and the exercise of British power elsewhere in the world has been dominant. All opposition to those in charge of the united British State has been neutralised, whether external or internal in origin, often by use of 'divide and rule' tactics. The unionist ideology, buttressed by pragmatic arguments, has been supported by appeals to resist incursions on British sovereignty by Brussels and by outbreaks of jingoism and reinforcement of national pride occasioned by victory in world wars and the 'successful' Falklands war. The national tabloid press, which is very extensively read, has been a willing accomplice in reinforcing such attitudes.

There is an implicit assumption too that a weakening of the bonds that tie the components of the British state together will work to the advantage of Britain's more powerful competitors, undermining British effectiveness on the world stage. According to this argument, a strong Britain is better equipped to resist any Franco-German conspiracy in Brussels or the escapades of any United States administration. Britain, despite its much reduced economic and political weight, must still have its own independent nuclear defence capability, larger than average standing armed forces, and its own seat on the United Nations Security Council. Applying this perspective, there is no real recognition that other large states have sought to and succeeded in drawing strength from the institutionalisation of their own internal regional diversity and needs.

Unionist ideology has combined happily with a mistrust of local government leadership and its integrity. Although all too many Westminster politicians have 'fallen short' in their personal lives or embarked upon foolish policy nostrums (the 'poll tax' fiasco of 1988-91 being a fine example), it is the vicissitudes of certain local councils (especially in Labour parts of London) and of fallen heroes such as Newcastle's T. Dan Smith that are best remembered. The British political élite (like the Irish political class) does not trust local government and local politicians, an attitude which conveniently feeds the trend towards even greater centralisation of power in London. Regional government and elected regional assemblies are depicted as introducing extra and unnecessary layers of bureaucracy. Arguments for greater accountability over the exercise of executive discretion are brushed aside. There is almost a pervasive attitude of fatalism about the efficacy of any reform of UK political institutions, not so surprising in view of the widely-perceived 'failures' of all health service and local government reforms since the 1960s.

Ideology and scepticism about the politics of regionalism have also found support from strong localist sentiment especially in parts of England, which is focussed on the traditional counties, with their long history and tradition. The county councils are expected to be the casualty of the new round of government reform in progress, in which case the way would be much clearer for establishing a regional tier of government at a later date.

Another unspoken factor at work is the fear felt by the Westminster-based political class concerning the creation of rival power bases and potential competitors in the political process. This was most graphically illustrated by the refusal of the Houses of Parliament to give any privileged access to its premises to the 81 elected members of the European Parliament for the first 11 years of their existence. The MEPs were seen as poaching on the constituency work of MPs and were, it seems, not to be encouraged or assisted in their work. Westminster has much the same self-interested approach to the possibility of delegating its work to and offering an alternative significant political career structure through new regional political institutions.

Although this analysis is not encouraging about regionalism in the United Kingdom, it has set out to show that regional issues are likely to return to the top of the political agenda especially if there is a change of government at Westminster. There are significant pressures within the political system in the United Kingdom which will force Parliament to take another hard look at the devolution options, and it is likely that any scheme adopted will have to have an English dimension to it in order to gain full political consent and legitimacy. Those who support the strengthening of political regionalism in Britain can continue to use the EC dimension as a lever on national government to persuade it to take account of regional policy needs and to put in place some appropriate regional administrative structures. But a more dramatic strategy, one much more difficult to achieve, would be for political parties in the United Kingdom to use the electoral system for Westminster elections to force the issue by uniting behind one 'regionalist' candidate in each constituency. The effect could be as dramatic as the sweeping from power of the Canadian Government in October 1993, when the governing party was left with a mere two seats in the legislature, but party competition and advantage is likely to get in the way of such a project, and the priority that would have to be given to demanding a new constitution and settlement in the UK is not yet sufficiently accepted. Failing this, those who would like to see a stronger regional tier of government will have to do more to win the argument among the general public by facing down the complaint that regionalism will lead to more bureaucracy and by restating the arguments for greater democratic control and accountability over existing government activities. There also needs to be a conscious attempt, especially on the part of those in local government, to build up regional institutions so as to encourage greater regional identification in England and to demonstrate the relevance and need for a regional dimension. Two obvious areas where more could be usefully done are in strategic planning at regional level, and economic development with the formation of more regional development agencies by local authorities. One example of regional cooperation on strategic planning questions is to be found in the SERPLAN organisation, a forum in which the planning officers of London boroughs and South-East English county councils develop policy and through which they lobby Whitehall. Since only one county council in England is exclusively controlled by the Conservatives there are important opportunities for the opposition parties to pursue a regional agenda through local government. There is little evidence that this is their intention, a measure perhaps of the more short-term focus of the political parties and of the low intensity of feeling in England on the regional dimension to politics.

Table 1: *Regional unemployment rates 1971-1993 (%)*

	1971	1979	1982	1986	1988	1993[1]
South East	2.2	2.7	7.0	8.5	5.2	10.2
South West	3.3	4.2	7.9	9.7	6.3	9.7
East Anglia	3.1	3.3	7.7	8.8	4.8	8.4
East Midlands	2.9	3.5	8.8	10.3	7.3	9.6
West Midlands	2.9	4.2	12.2	12.9	8.5	11.0
Yorkshire and Humberside	3.7	4.4	10.8	12.8	9.5	10.3
North West	3.8	5.4	12.4	14.4	10.6	10.7
North	5.5	6.9	13.6	15.7	11.8	12.3
Wales	4.3	5.7	12.4	14.4	10.3	10.4
Scotland	5.7	6.2	11.7	13.8	11.4	9.6
Northern Ireland	7.1	8.1	14.7	18.3	16.3	14.1
All of UK	2.8	4.3	9.9	11.5	8.0	10.3

[1] September only
Source: Department of Employment

References

Audit Commission (1991), *A Rough Guide to Europe: Local Authorities and the EC*, London, HMSO.

Bogdanor, V. (1979), *Devolution*, Harmondsworth, Penguin.

Butler, D. and D. Kavanagh (1988), *The British General Election of 1987*, London, Macmillan.

Butler, D. and D. Kavanagh, (1992), *The British General Election of 1992*, London, Macmillan.

Butt Philip, A. (1975), *The Welsh Question*, Cardiff, University of Wales Press.

Butt Philip, A. (1978), *Creating New Jobs*, London, Policy Studies Institute.

Capon, B., *The Times*, 2 November 1993.

Department of Employment, *Preliminary Results from the 1987 Labour Force Survey* (1988), Table 4.

Department of Trade and Industry, *DTI - The Department of Enterprise*, London, HMSO, Cmnd. 278, January 1988.

Hanham, H. (1969), *Scottish Nationalism*, London, Faber.

Hencke, D, 'Welfare cuts hit poorest areas worst', *The Guardian*, 20 September 1993.

House of Lords Select Committee on the European Communities, *European Regional Development Fund*, 23rd Report of Session 1983-84, HL Paper 274. pp. xxix–xxxii.

House of Lords Select Committee on the European Communities, *Reform of the Structural Funds*, 14th Report of Session 1987-88, HL Paper 82, pp. 18–19.

Moores, B., J. Rhodes and P. Tyler (1986), *The Effects of Government Regional Policy*, London, Department of Trade and Industry, HMSO.

Report of the Royal Commission on Local Government in England (1969), Cmnd. 4040, London, HMSO.

Report of the Royal Commission on the Constitution (1973), Vols I and II, Cmnd. 5460, London, HMSO.

Rose, R. (1982), *Understanding the United Kingdom*, Harlow, Longman.

Smith, D. (1989), *North and South: Britain's Growing Divide*, Harmondsworth, Penguin.

Tighe, C., 'Portsmouth to compete for EC aid', *Financial Times*, 12 October 1993.

White, M. (1993a), 'Confusion on urban renewal supremos', *The Guardian*, 15 October 1993.

White, M. (1993b), 'Regions regain planning clout', *The Guardian*, 5 November 1993.

Willman, J. and T. Burt, 'Business help sought in urban revival plan', *Financial Times*, 1 November 1993.

Wintour, P., 'Whitehall seeks EC aid for depressed South-East', *The Guardian*, 12 October 1993.

Epilogue

For many years, regional policy has been a major concern of the European Community, not least because it was seen as a necessary concomitant to the gradual progress towards economic and monetary union. The introduction of three so-called structural funds - the guidance section of the fund financing the Common Agricultural Policy and the European Social Fund in the early 1960s, and the European Regional Development Fund in 1974, set in place the framework for the support of regional activity across the Community. The modernisation of agriculture, the reconversion of declining industries, urban development, major infrastructure projects, have all benefited from the resources thus made available.

In recent years the regional question has assumed an ever greater importance within the policies of the European Community. Since 1989 the financial impact of the structural funds had been significantly increased by changes to the rules governing intervention. Furthermore, the new designation of European Union in 1993 seems set coincidentally to formalise the status of regions at a supra-national level for the first time, as the Maastricht Treaty enshrines the principle of a Committee of the Regions. Although its role is to be no more than consultative, and in spite of the fact that, as we have seen, its composition provokes sharp differences of emphasis in member states, the proposed Committee of the Regions will provide a forum for the co-ordinated discussion of regional priorities and for the distribution of resources.

It should not be assumed, however (and the preceding chapters make this abundantly clear), that the regional question owes its contemporary significance to a perhaps belated, if growing, awareness of its importance on the part of the EC. The modern history of almost all the countries under discussion reveals a consistent theme, which is the need to establish and maintain a balance between the requirements of the unitary state and the regional aspirations of its constituent parts. Of course, the flame of regional ambition burns more brightly in some places than in others, and its strength grows and subsides with the passage of time. By the same token, some states have been better able, indeed even obliged, to reach a satisfactory accommodation with their regions. Thus, Germany has its very origins as a state in the assumption that central and regional governments can establish an equilibrium of power and responsibility. France, Spain and Italy, in contrast, have yet to arrive at settlements of their particular region-state dilemmas - dilemmas which present themselves with varying degrees of urgency. Belgium is in the process of resolving its own regional problems by recourse to a tentative federalism the results of which cannot yet be foreseen. As far as the United Kingdom is concerned, the abortive devolution debates of the 1970s, followed by a decade and more of increased centralisation of power in Whitehall lead, perhaps misleadingly, to the conclusion that the regional question has run out of steam. Yet here, as elsewhere, there is evidence that the commitment of citizens to existing political structures and institutions has faltered. Talk of a crisis of legitimacy of those institutions does not seem out of place in the UK, or France, or Italy. In Germany, too, electoral participation is at a low ebb. The outcome of the Italian Parliamentary elections in March 1994 and the European elections three months later offer no indication that the crisis has lessened.

It is in this context that the regional question assumes a new vitality. Left to their own devices, regional structures can achieve little. In a wider, European framework, linked together into networks of co-operation and support, regional identities are perhaps starting to assert themselves, their traditions and values, their cultural and economic strengths, with increased confidence. It remains to be seen whether, in the process, they can rekindle, within the larger edifice of the European Union, the spark of commitment, allegiance and participation among the people of western Europe.

Bibliography

Adamson, D. L. (1991), *Class, Ideology and the Nation*, Cardiff, University of Wales Press.

Allum, P. A. (1973), *Italy: Republic without Government?* New York, Norton.

Bagnasco, A. (1977), *Tre Italie. La problematica territoriale dello sviluppo italiano*, Bologna, Il Mulino.

Benko, G. and A. Lipietz (eds.) (1992), *Les Régions qui gagnent: districts et réseaux: les nouveaux paradigmes de la géographie économique*, Paris, PUF.

Bogdanor, V. (1979), *Devolution*, Harmondsworth, Penguin.

Borkenhagen, F., *et al* (eds.) (1992), *Die Deutschen Länder in Europa*, Baden-Baden, Nomos.

Brand, J. (1978), *The National Movement in Scotland*, London, Routledge and Kegan Paul.

Braudel, F. (1986), *L'Identité de la France: espace et histoire*, Paris, Arthaud-Flammarion.

Brongniart, P. (1971), *La Région en France*, Paris, Colin.

Bundesrat (1989), *Vierzig Jahre Bundesrat*, Baden-Baden, Nomos.

Bundesrat (1991), *Handbuch des Bundesrates*, Munich, Beck.

Butt Philip, A. (1975), *The Welsh Question*, Cardiff, University of Wales Press.

Cammelli, M. 'Regioni e rappresentanza degli interessi: il caso italiano', *Stato e mercato* , N. 2. August 1990, pp. 151-200.

Chubb, J. (1990), *Patronage, Power and Poverty in Southern Italy*, Cambridge, Cambridge University Press.

Clark, M. (1983), *Modern Italy 1871-1982*, London and New York, Longman.

Cole, J. and F. Cole (1993), *The Geography of the European Community*, London and New York, Routledge.

CSS (1991), *Italy today: social picture and trends*: 1990, Milan, Angeli.

Dayries, J.-J. and M. Dayries (1978), *La Régionalisation*, Paris, PUF.

Dematteis, G. (1989), 'Regioni geografiche, articolazione territoriale degli interessi e regioni istituzionali', *Stato e mercato*, 27.

Drevet, J.-F. (1988), *1992-2000: les régions françaises entre l'Europe et le déclin*, Paris, Souffles.

Drevet, J.-F. (1991), *La France et l'Europe des régions*, Paris, Syros.

Feijo, R. C. (1989), 'State, nation and regional diversity in Portugal: an overview', in R. Herr and J. H. R. Polt (eds.), *Iberian Identity: Essays on the Nature of Identity in Portugal and Spain*, Berkeley, Institute of International Studies.

Fitzmaurice, J. (1984), 'Belgium: Reluctant Federalism', *Parliamentary Affairs*, 37, pp. 418-433.

Frenkel, M, (1984/86), *Föderalismus und Bundesstaat* (2 vols.), Bern/Frankfurt.

Fuà, G. and C. Zacchia (eds.) (1983), *Industrializzazione senza fratture*, Bologna, Il Mulino.

Ginsborg, P. (1990), *A History of Contemporary Italy: Society and Politics*, London, Penguin.

Gravier, J. F. (1947), *Paris et le désert français*, Paris, Portulan.

Gravier, J. F. (1970), *La Question régionale*, Paris, Flammarion.

Gruber, A. (1986), *La Décentralisation et les institutions administratives*, Paris, Colin.

Hasquin, H. (1982), *Historiographie et politique: Essai sur l'histoire de la Belgique et la Wallonie* (2nd edition), Charleroi, Institut Jules Destrée.

Haycraft, J. ((1985), *Italian Labyrinth*, Harmondsworth, Penguin Books.

Hesse, K. (1984), *Grundzüge des Verfassungsrechts des Bundesrepublik Deutschland*, Karlsruhe, Müller.

Hine, D. (1993), *Governing Italy. The politics of Bargained Pluralism*, Oxford, Clarendon Press.

Hrbek, R. and U. Thaysen (eds.) (1986), *Die Deutschen Länder und die Europäischen Gemeinschaften*, Baden-Baden, Nomos.

Huggett, F. E. (1969), *Modern Belgium*, London, Pall Mall Press.

Keating, M. (1988), *State and Regional nationalism: Territorial Politics and the European State*, London, Harvester Wheatsheaf.

Keating, M. and P. Hainsworth (1986), *Decentralization and Change in Contemporary France*,

Kossmann-Putto, J. A. and E. H. Kossmann (1987), *The Low Countries: History of the Northern and Southern Netherlands*, Flanders, Flemish Netherlands Foundation.

Lafont, R. (1971), *Décoloniser en France*, Paris, Gallimard.

Lanversin, J. de, A. Lanza and F. Zitouni (1989), *La Région et l'Aménagement du territoire dans la décentralisation*, 4th. edition, Paris, Economica.

Laufer, H. and F. Pilz (1973), *Föderalismus*, Munich.

Lehmbruch, G. (1976), *Parteienwettbewerb im Bundesstaat*, Stuttgart, Kohlhammer.

Leonardi, R., R. Nanetti and R. Putnam (1987), 'Italy: Territorial Politics in the Postwar Years: The Case of Regional Reform', *West European Politics*, 10:4, 88-107.

Mack Smith, D. (ed.) (1968), *The Making of Italy*, New York, Harper and Row.

Mannheimer, R. (ed.) (1991), *La Lega lombarda*, Milan, Feltrinelli.

Mény, Y. (1974), *Centralisation et décentralisation dans le débat politique français (1945-1969)*, Paris, Pichon and Durand-Auzias.

Morisi, M. (ed.) (1987), *Regioni e rappresentanza politica*, Milan, Angeli.

Mughan, A. (1983), 'Accommodation or Diffusion in the Management of Linguistic Conflict in Belgium', *Political Studies* (1983), XXXI, pp. 434-451.

Nairn, T. (1977), *The Break-up of Britain: Crisis and Neo-Nationalism*, London, NLB.

Nanetti, R. (1988), *Growth and Territorial Policies. The Italian Model of Social Capitalism*, London and New York, Pinter Publishers.

Nyman, O. (1960), *Der westdeutsche Föderalismus*, Stockholm.

Osmond, J. (ed.) (1985), *The National Question Again*, Llandysul, Gomer Press.

Ossenbühl, F. (ed.) (1990), *Föderalismus und Regionalismus in Europa*, Baden-Baden, Nomos.

Pagenkopf, H. (1981), *Der Finanzausgleich im Bundesstaat*, Stuttgart, Kohlhammer.

Perrineau, P. (1987), *Régions: le baptême des urnes*, Paris, Pedone.

Pisani, E. (1969), *La Région... pour quoi faire? ou le triomphe des jacondins*, Paris, Calmann Lévy.

Podbielski, G. (1974), *Italy: Development and Crisis in the Post-war Economy*, Oxford, Clarendon Press.

Putnam, R. D. (with R. Leonardi and R. Nanetti) (1993), *Making Democracy Work. Civic Traditions in Modern Italy*, Princeton, New Jersey, Princeton university Press.

Putnam, R. D., R. Leonardi and R. Nanetti (1985), *La pianta e le radici*, Bologna, Il Mulino.

Quartermaine, L. and J. Pollard (eds.) (1985), *Italy Today: Patterns of Life and Politics*, Exeter, University of Exeter.

Ragionieri, E. (1979), *Politica e amministrazione nella storia dell'Italia unita*, Rome, Editori Riuniti.

Report of the Royal Commission on the Constitution, Vols. I and II, Cmnd. 5460 (1973), London, HMSO.

Rhodes, R. A. W. and V. Wright (1987), 'Introduction', *West European Politics*, vol. 10, no. 4 (Special Issue on 'Tensions in the Territorial Politics of Western Europe'), pp. 1-20.

Rokkan, S. and D. W. Urwin (eds.) (1982), *The Politics of Territorial Identity: Studies in European Regionalism*, London, Sage.

Rose, R. (1982), *Understanding the United Kingdom: The Territorial Dimension*, Harlow, Longman.

Ruffilli, R. (1971), *La questione regionale dall'unificazione alla dittatura* , Milan, Giuffrè.

Sampson, A. (1992), *The Essential Anatomy of Britain: Democracy in Crisis*, London, Hodder and Stoughton.

Sassoon, D. (1986), *Contemporary Italy*, London, Longmans.

Schmidt, V. A. (1990), *Democratizing France: the political and administrative history of decentralization*, Cambridge, CUP.

Senelle, R. (1987), *The Reform of the Belgian State*, Vol. IV, Brussels, Ministry of Foreign Affairs and External Trade (Memo from Belgium No. 196).

Smith, D. (1989), *North and South: Britain's Economic, Social and Political Divide*, London, Penguin.

Spotts, F. and T. Wieser (1986), *Italy, a Difficult Democracy,* Cambridge, Cambridge University Press.

Tarrow, S. (1977), *Between Center and Periphery: Grassroots Politicians in Italy and France*, New Haven, Yale University Press.

Thomas, P. (1990), 'Belgium's North–South Divide and the Walloon Regional Problem', *Geography*, No. 326, Vol. 75, Part I (January 1990), pp. 36–50.

Uhrich, R. (1987), *La France inverse: les régions en mutation*, Paris, Economica.

Vos, L. (1993), 'Shifting nationalism: Belgians, Flemings and Walloons', in M. Teich and R. Porter (eds.), *The National Question in Europe in Historical Context*, Cambridge, Cambridge University Press.

Weber, E. (1977), *Peasants into Frenchmen: the modernization of rural France 1870-1914*, London, Chatto and Windus.

Wilke, D. and B. Schulte (1990), *Der Bundesrat. Entwicklung des föderalen Verfassungsorgans*, Darmstadt, Wissenschaftliche Buchgesellschaft.

Wils, L. (1993), 'Belgium on the Path to Equal Language Rights up to 1939', in *Ethnic Groups and Language Rights (Comparative Studies on Governments and Non-Dominant Ethnic Groups in Europe, 1850-1940*, Vol. III), Dartmouth, New York University Press.

Witte, E. *et al* (1984), *Le Bilinguisme en Belgique: le cas de Bruxelles*, Brussels, Editions de l'Université de Bruxelles.

intellect

EUROPEAN STUDIES SERIES

Humour and History

Presented by Keith Cameron

To write on the theme of humour and history is in many ways to undertake a study of the whole of mankind. Aristotle felt that laughter was a distinctive trait of humanity and one which distinguished man from the animals. On the other hand, the very existence of man could be considered a 'joke'. The aim of this book is to examine some of the facets of humour in its broadest sense, one which encompasses satire, irony and ridicule. In short, man's attitude to laughter and his use of it to influence public opinion.

The contributors to the volume were asked as their brief to study within their various fields (psychology, philosophy, drama, theology, sociology and the humanities) uses of, or theories about, humour. The result is a fascinating insight into the role humour has played in various European cultures throughout their history.

CHAPTERS INCLUDE:

- •Humour and History
- •Psychoanalysis and Humour
- •Humour and Philosophy
- •Humour in the Bible
- •Abusive Criticism and the Criticism of Abuse
- •Paradigms of Power: Roman Emperors in Roman Satire
- •L'Esprit Gaulois: Humour and National Mythology
- •The Devil and Comedy
- •Magna Farta: Walpole, Fielding and the Licensing Act of 1737
- •Irony and the Historical

THE PRESENTER

Dr Keith Cameron is Professor of Mediaeval French Literature at the University of Exeter. He studied French with German at the University of Exeter; education at the University of Cambridge; phonetics, linguistics and sixteenth-century literature at the University of Rennes (France). He is author of many publications and Editor of *Computer Assisted Language Learning: an International Journal* (Swets).

PRICE: £14.95 PAPERBACK

ISBN 1-871516-80-3

intellect
EUROPEAN STUDIES SERIES

The Nation: Myth or Reality
Edited by Keith Cameron

Within the confines of a political nation state there can be subdivisions which divide the larger whole into smaller groups, whether ethnically, by language or by regional culture. This collection of papers looks at the various ways in which a national character is shaped and defined as well as examining how boundaries are created. In a Europe which is attempting to create unifying forces across an enormous diversity of peoples the concept of nationhood is once again due for re-examination. Many of the states looking for closer integration were themselves only created from loose federations in the last century.

It is in this context that the contributors to this volume discuss the concept of nation from a wide variety of perspectives and disciplines.

THE EDITOR

Dr Keith Cameron is Professor of Mediaeval French Literature at the University of Exeter. He studied French with German at the University of Exeter; education at the University of Cambridge; phonetics, linguistics and sixteenth-century literature at the University of Rennes (France). He is author of many publications and Editor of *Computer Assisted Language Learning: an International Journal* (Swets).

CONTENTS

- Anglo-Saxon Origins: the reality of the myth - Malcolm Todd
- State and Nation: Germany since reunification – Mark Blacksel
- Anglo-Welshness: the semantics of hyphenation – Diane Davies
- English and French poetic languages compared – Martin Sorrell
- The elastic nation or when is a category not a category – Lynn Williams
- The rise and fall of the Reithian Sunday: 1936-1959 – Christopher McCullough
- The Nation, a real myth – David Braund

PRICE: £9.95 PAPERBACK

ISBN 1-871516-85-4

ORDER NOW FROM YOUR LOCAL BOOKSELLER OR WRITE TO:
intellect
108-110 London Road, Oxford OX3 9AW, UK.

intellect

EUROPEAN STUDIES SERIES

Women in European Theatre

Elizabeth Woodrough

Very few books have been published on women's theatre and even fewer that do not take a radically feminist viewpoint. Uniquely, this book does exactly that, through considering the written playscript and performance as of equal importance, avoiding the one-sided emphasis on the written text, which has been identified as a problem area for women's theatre in search of a history.

Women in European Theatre is both a study of women as writers and performers in Britain, France, Germany and Italy, and a study of conditions in the theatre as they affect women from the 17th century to the 1970s. It also draws attention to a number of plays by women which have never appeared in print and some which have only just been republished after centuries of neglect.

The book is dedicated to the memory of Lizzie Howe, author of *The First Restoration Actresses* (CUP 1992) who was tragically murdered at an Open University summer school in 1992. The book contains a previously unpublished article by her on the sexuality of actresses on the English Restoration stage.

THE EDITOR

Elizabeth Woodrough is a lecturer in the Department of French at the University of Exeter.

CONTENTS

PRICE: £9.95 PAPERBACK

ISBN 1-871516-86-2

ORDER NOW FROM YOUR LOCAL BOOKSELLER OR WRITE TO:
intellect
108-110 London Road, Oxford OX3 9AW, UK.

intellect

EUROPEAN
STUDIES
SERIES

Children and Propaganda

Judith K Proud

Childhood has featured as a significant topos in works of propaganda throughout Europe in many different socio-political contexts. Nostalgia for lost youth, for an innocent golden age, whether individual or collective, is a theme often capitalised upon by the writer of propaganda, but governments have also exploited childhood in a much more cynical and far-reaching manner, by making it an important target, not only for social conditioning through education, but also for political and racial indoctrination through the less overtly didactic medium of children's literature.

This volume brings together three studies which demonstrate how the everyday literature of youth has been subverted at key points in twentieth-century European history, to promote the ideologies of a dominant political regime. Concentrating primarily on the specific area of children's fiction, *Children and Propaganda* focuses on the propaganda writing of Vichy France; the cult of seafaring in Nazi Germany; and images of empire and decolonisation in France between 1930 and 1962. Each study analyses a significant body of primary material, identifying thematic and formal paradigms characterising the field of investigation. In addition to close textual study, works are located within the wider contexts and discourses that shaped their production, dissemination and reception, giving the volume a broad, cross-disciplinary range of appeal.

THE AUTHORS

Judith K Proud is a lecturer in French at University College Swansea and has previously carried out research for the British Library at Oxford University.

PRICE: £14.95 PAPERBACK

ISBN 1-871516-83-8

ORDER NOW FROM YOUR LOCAL BOOKSELLER OR WRITE TO:
intellect
108-110 London Road, Oxford OX3 9AW, UK.

intellect

EUROPEAN
STUDIES
SERIES

The European Community – Culture and Society

Professor John Fletcher

Broad in scope, this books deals with cultural and social aspects of European integration, focusing on Europe as a cultural idea (and ideal); cultural policy and action; the media; immigration management; changing social structures; welfare policy, and the social charter.

While recognising the momentous changes (still evolving) within the community the author argues that it has for a long time had a logic and therefore dynamic of its own, and it will not be stopped in its tracks for long. With this in mind the book looks at the achievements of the EC, and its failures, and attempts to provide answers to a range of important questions such as: How far have Europeans a sense of identity, and how can that sense be fostered? How do people in the different states of the Community think of themselves, and of their fellow-peoples? Can the EC develop the European ideal without - on the one hand - weakening the identity of individual states or provinces within it, and - on the other - without creating an entity as chauvinistic and exclusive as in the past nation-states have tended to be? These questions are answered in the context of a range of topics including cultural policy, cultural institutions and the media; education and youth; women and Europe; environment and immigration. The book concludes with a chapter on permanence and change in Europe where the author looks at the welfare state, the concept of a 'social charter', class structures in Europe and the social chapter of the Maastricht treaty and the controversy it has provoked.

THE AUTHOR

Professor John Fletcher is Professor of European Literature at the University of East Anglia, Norwich.

PRICE: £14.95 PAPERBACK

ISBN 1-871516-81-1

ORDER NOW FROM YOUR LOCAL BOOKSELLER OR WRITE TO:
intellect
108-110 London Road, Oxford OX3 9AW, UK.